D0927586

Additional Books by the Author

Diamond in the Rough

DNA: Who's Your Daddy?

Don't Birth an Ishmael in the Waiting Room

From the Pit to the Prison to the Palace

It's Time to Come Out of Lo-debar

Mercy and the Sufficiency of Grace

Midnight

Perceive and Receive

Praise Worship and the Spirit of Prophecy

The Power of Persistent Prayer

Great Women

Fidel M. Donaldson

"The Lord gives the command; The women who proclaim the good tidings are a great host"

New American Standard Bible

Great Women

ISBN 978-1-64007-783-6

LCCN 2017935889

Cover Design & Layout by D'Edge Media / dedgemedia.com
Printed in the United States of America

ACKNOWLEDGEMENTS

This book is dedicated to my mother Monica Donaldson, my wife for life Lady Paulette Donaldson and the Great Women who have and continue to enrich my life.

Contents

Contents

FOREWORD—THE HELP

Beside every great man you will find a great woman. WHY? Because it was God's idea to place her there. A woman was never man's idea, according to Genesis 2:21-22: "So the Lord God caused the man to fall into a deep sleep; and while he was sleeping, he took one of the man's ribs and then closed up the place with flesh. Then the Lord God made a woman from the rib he had taken out of the man, and he brought her to the man." Creating a woman was clearly God's concept. God defined and identified her as man's help; to specify, a "help meet." Many may not think of the word help as a compliment, but if you think about it the word help is associated with someone with the T.A.S.K (talents, abilities, skills and knowledge) to make things easier or less difficult; someone who contributes, relieves, serves, gives, cooperates, assists, advises, benefits, comforts, corrects, guides, lifts, supports, nourishes or provides whatever is necessary to accomplish or satisfy a need. WOW, if God created and equipped a single individual to do all these things, that individual is indeed a blessing or better yet, she is a Great Woman. Proverbs 18:22 says "He who finds a wife finds what is good and receives favor from the Lord." God was saying—when a man finds a wife he finds help—the one source God created other than himself, to help meet the needs of a man. The word help is fully loaded; this is why it is a gift of the Spirit.

Not everyone has the gift, temperament or patience to help. Nevertheless, when God designed a woman he made that to be a part of her DNA. Many men will go to a friend, get a second job or sit in their car in silence when there is a problem rather than share that problem or concern with their spouse. Men do this because they have been taught that the woman is the weaker vessel and men are the head. These statements may be biblical, but at times they are taken out of context. When God designed the woman, the man was asleep so man really does not know all that God included when He created her. To be honest, the woman does not know either. What she does know is, when her husband comes to her with a need, she intuitively knows what to do.

In this book, Apostle Fidel goes beyond the surface to explore and search for diamonds in the rough and hidden treasure. He looks carefully at what each of these Great Women did, along with the character they possessed, to unveil the qualities of a Great Woman.

At first glance, this may not seem like a relevant use of time, but women are birthers and replenishers; they make the world go around. Today, some women are devaluing themselves, being abused, not stepping forward, not rising to the occasion and not taking their place in society because they fail to realize how great they really are. They also fail to realize how the smallest task has changed lives, nations and started historical movements. This book highlights the characteristics of true greatness.

According to Don Yaeger, the Author of Greatness: "Greatness is the product of choices; Greatness overcomes; Greatness lifts and recognizes those around it; Greatness has vision; Greatness is humble and Greatness does what others will not" (2011). Great Women packages the very essence of the woman and how God's strategic design of a "help meet" has greatly impacted men, children, education, government, religion, the economy and every other major pillar in our society. Women are often considered the minority, but if you walk in any church, on any given day, they dominate in attendance and are clearly the majority. The work place is the complete opposite only because man created a glass ceiling saying that the woman has no place there. Yet, the very same man that made these rules was breastfed, raised and educated by a woman. In 2017, the battle for equality between men and women continues, but women no longer need to fight to be great because greatness is on the inside of them. This year a phenomenal movie called **HIDDEN FIGURES** was released; it is clear that there is now an awareness of the greatness of women. If women of all colors, creeds and nationalities would understand who they are, the qualities they possess and most importantly who designed them, their gifts would make room for them. Even if they did not know what their gifts were, simply being **THE HELP** is enough to be what God created them to be and that is **GREAT WOMEN!**

Dr. Monica Hardy
Love, Peace & Joy Ministry, Visionary & Pastor
Kingdom Scholastic Center of Excellence, Founder & Provost
Dr. Monica Hardy Ministries, CEO, Editor/Book Doctor & Author
Jacksonville, FL

PREFACE

"A woman is the full circle. Within her is the power to create, nurture and transform."- Diane Mariechild

This book was birthed out of a message I ministered during The Greater Power Conference in Miami, FL. I always endeavor to seek the Lord for the specific word He desires me to teach or preach when I am invited to speak. Sometimes, He gives me the subject for the message in advance and sometimes He gives it to me the day before. I was scheduled to speak on a Saturday morning and the Holy Spirit uploaded the subject to me the day before. The subject He gave me was, The Ministry of Women. It was quite fitting because the conference attendees were predominantly women.

The Honorable Bishop TD Jakes wrote a bestselling book titled, Woman Thou Art Loosed. The success resulted in a movie and many sold-out conferences. The question I now ask is what were the women loosed to do? My answer is they were loosed to be **GREAT!** Women were loosed from everything that yoked, shackled, or stifled their potential for greatness. They were loosed to be the Great Women they were created to be and that is women with dominion, power and authority.

As I began to do research into the lives of the women of the Bible, I started to see a portrait of greatness. Their greatness did not stem from the fact that they were born into privilege or they were a part of some aristocracy—quite the contrary, most of them manifested greatness for the Lord and impacted their society because of their fortitude and their resilience. I have always had the utmost respect for women, but my study and preparation for the conference took my respect and admiration for women to another dimension. Why women, you ask? Because women have something men do not, a **WOMB** (women overcoming momentous burdens). Men plant but Women conceive, carry, birth and nurture. Although a child is not considered a burden, the bearing and birthing process requires someone who can endure pain.

In this book, you will not only see and value the greatness of women like the Daughters of Zelophehad who refused to allow tradition and legalism to hinder them from receiving their inheritance; or Hannah the silent prayer warrior who rose above the torment of her nemesis Peninnah to birth out a Prophet, Priest, and Judge named Samuel; or the Widow of Zarephath who gave up her last meal to sustain the Prophet Elijah; but you will also see the greatness in YOU because their life stories will reflect what you are already doing or have the potential to do. Each and every day, I encounter Great Women or women who have the potential to be great, but some lack awareness and confidence. In other words, they literally do not realize that what they have done, are doing, or have the potential to do, are the defining factors and key principles for greatness. The women in the Bible coined greatness; their lives are a mirror that women today should look into and see themselves.

Many lives were transformed by the power of God because of the altruism and unselfishness of these 'Sheroes'. Those women impacted the lives of individuals who lived in their locale and changed the lives of generations who came after them; their stories made it into the canon of the Bible. My goal in writing this book is not simply to recount, rehash, or regurgitate the stories of the Great Women—but to inspire, to encourage, and to motivate the many women and men who will read this book to emulate the Great Women of the Bible. It is my desire for their stories to give you the strength and motivation to rise above every roadblock and obstacle, so every stumbling block can be used as a stepping stone to greatness.

My good friend and sister, in the Lord, Pansy Rose, sent me an inspiring message when I asked her to pray for this book. Her words blessed me so much, I felt compelled to put it here. Pansy wrote: "Shalom Apostle. The Lord is using you through the inspiration of the Holy Spirit to reach women in every sphere of the globe. Even as you are calling women to a higher place in the Lord, you are helping us to recognize that we are more than what society has labeled us. We are more than pretty faces and objects of lust, but we are fearfully and wonderfully made. God made us special—intuitive, nurturing, sensitive, faithful to His Kingdom, and so much more.

You will further help women to recognize and realize their God-ordained roles while respecting the headship of the men God has placed over them. I pray that inspiration will continue to flow and the Lord will strengthen you through the process. This one will be even greater, Apostle. Agape Shalom!" From your lips to Abba Father's Ears, Minister Rose; be it unto me, according to thy word!

Section One

TRIUMPH OVER TRAGEDY

Paulette Donaldson

You Must Be Able to Discern the Greatness in the GOOD THING You Have Found and Not Allow a Spirit of Insecurity to Cause You to Stifle Her Greatness. If You Allow That to Happen, You Will Not Be Able to Obtain the Favor From the Lord That is Promised to You When You Find a Good Woman.

PAULETTE DONALDSON—MY WIFE FOR LIFE!

ehind every great man stands no woman. There is no greater man than the man that can acknowledge the woman standing right next to him. —Rachel Wolchin

As I embarked on the journey of writing this book—I spoke with my wife Paulette about the feeling I had of this book being a great blessing to many. Before I told her the name of the book, she thought I was going to title it, the Women of the Bible. When I informed her that the title would be, Great Women; she responded by looking me straight in the eyes and said—"I'm a great woman, am I in the book?" My immediate response came with a smile, as I said to her, "of course; a book called Great Women would not be complete without including the two greatest women in my life—my mother and my wife." I bless God for my mother, Monica Donaldson. She sacrificed greatly to get her seven children to America from very humble beginnings in Kingston, Jamaica, so we could have a better education and better economic opportunities. She worked the three to eleven shift at Memorial Sloan Kettering Hospital and utilized the seamstress skills taught to her by her mom, Edith Maxwell, to give us a better life; Like Great Women all over the world, she sacrificed her time, energy and finances for her children.

Words do not seem adequate to describe a real wife, specifically, my wife. She is the woman who has epitomized the words found in the marital vow: "In sickness and in health, for richer or for poorer, 'til death do us part." She is a true and rare gem, more specifically, a diamond. As the diamond is formed in the intense heat and pressure, is cut and polished prior to being placed on display, my wife endured great heat and pressure, cutting and polishing, by standing strong with me during very difficult times, seasons and circumstances. I can only imagine how she must have felt, many years ago, when a woman in our neighborhood approached her and told her I was arrested in England and was given a life sentence. At the time, she had our three young children ages 5, 3 and 1; she must have felt forsaken and abandoned wondering how she was going to make it without me.

My wife has never been a woman of many words, but she's undoubtedly a woman of deep faith in the Lord Jesus Christ. Paulette is a praying woman who is deeply committed to family, especially her children. As I have matriculated in life, "Greatness" is not measured by how successful we are in life; it is not measured by the amount of education we have; or the amount of material things we acquire. However, greatness is measured by our ability to help others while we are dealing with our own trials. During the long season of my imprisonment and the deep heartache and pain thrust upon my wife by my reckless actions, which led to my incarceration; she committed herself to praying for me, and to making sure the children received the best care she could possibly give them.

When I was first incarcerated Paulette had no idea how much time I would serve, although not long after, she was erroneously told I was given a life sentence. I did not call or write home right away because I knew she was justifiably angry and disappointed. She had warned me not to leave for England with drugs prior to the ill-fated trip. As a matter of fact, I can still remember the day she said, "Fidel, God does not want you to go." I was so resolute in my desire and plans to make the trip that I ignored her pleadings and ignored the divine sign given to me by God, when I could not find my passport. Some may call the ominous warning female intuition, but she was being led by the Holy Spirit. I thank God that I did not receive a life sentence, but I did receive a lengthy sentence of eight years while facing indictment in the United States under the Rico Laws for being a part of a drug ring.

While my experience was unimaginably horrible, my wife's experience was equally horrifying and often underestimated. My wife and children were not locked up, but they also served the same sentence. Those were critical times for her and the children. To enumerate, Paulette had to relocate often for survival; she had to push the shopping cart full of clothes in the snow with the children in tow because there was no transportation nor was there a washer and dryer; she had to apply for government assistance (i.e., food stamps); she had to deal with the shame, embarrassment and whispers; she had to deal with the children's lack of understanding, which manifested through their behaviors; and she had to deal with her own heart, mind and emotions.

Paulette Donaldson

By the grace of God she proved herself to be a Great Woman, a Great Wife and a Great Mother—she made the necessary sacrifices to keep the household together until God brought me back to our family.

HELP MEET

From the Genesis of creation, this is what Almighty God, the Creator of the heavens and the earth, has spoken concerning man: "And the Lord God said, It is not good that the man should be alone; I will make him an help meet for him" (Genesis 2:18). The Jamieson, Fausset & Brown Commentary has this to say about the term "Help Meet" [Hebrew, kenegdo] - literally, 'as over against,' 'according to his front presence' - i.e., corresponding to, his counterpart-one like himself in form and constitution, disposition, and affections, and altogether suitable to his nature and wants. A friend and Kingdom colleague, John Feinstein, gave me great insight on the term 'Help Meet' Brother John said, "And He made woman to be azar kenegdo. The word azar is from the Hebrew for help, so translating it, 'to help,' is right. Neged is the preposition against." The prefix 'k' makes it 'as against' The suffix 'o' makes it 'as against him,' referring to the man.

So we have a help 'as against him' that God chose to make for man. Maybe the translators didn't know what to do with this strange expression of intended revelation, so they just used the word 'meet,' meaning whatever God thought must be appropriate, that must be what He made.

However, my interpretation presupposes or reveals a kind of oppositional-complementary relationship between man and woman as suggested in the term *against*." In Chinese philosophy, yin and yang describe how opposite forces are interdependent in the natural world. In the ABC Etymological Dictionary of Old Chinese, Axel Schuessler defines yin and yang as opposite forces that are actually complementary and interconnected because they give rise to each other as they interrelate to one another. We know man and woman are in many ways opposites. They are opposites in how they see things, in what they emphasize about family and relationships and purpose. However, oppositionality is not to be taken as a negative. In Taoism, yin and yang are described as two halves that together make a complete whole.

Oppositionality engenders complementarity which brings about harmony and balance. Examples of yin and yang are male and female, night and day, cold and hot, sun and moon, active and passive, etc. We see a woman as bringing balance to a man and a man as adding balance to a woman. Where did we get this word 'balance'? It goes back to a device used since antiquity of two weights, called counterweights because they exert force in opposition. When the two counter-weights are of the same weight they create what we call a balance. When one of them is heavier than the other we have imbalance. The mystery of God's creation is that in such a way He would so bless man and in doing so bless woman. What does this speak into our husband and wife relationships and our understanding of that dynamic? Woe to the husband who does not listen to his wife. He forfeits God's provision. Woe to the woman who does not listen to her husband. She forfeits God's provision to her. Together they are one and therefore complete.

Do we see such a dynamic elsewhere in God's order of things? "Iron sharpens iron," but not without friction, opposite forces, and pressure which creates heat. Do we have heated discussions? We are not out of God's order. Do we listen? The iron is actually getting sharper, not just hotter. Is a healthy marriage one without friction? Not in the best of cases, if anything dynamic is to happen, not if the man is to grow or the woman is to grow. Solomon said he saw that all things under heaven are the result of rivalry between a man and his brother. There is this side of life which can be healthy in what we call cooperation or unhealthy in what we call war. The activity of iron sharpening iron is to be managed carefully, so this godly activity does not spill over into the ungodly.

Kudos to Brother John for sharing this because it helps us to understand that friction between husband and wife should not lead them to the divorce court, but should be something used to strengthen their union. John's explanation has given me greater insight into the term, Help Meet. God did not create woman solely to help man, He created her to bring balance to his life. So, without woman, man is not only in a state of being alone, he is in a state of imbalance.

A man of wisdom should not look to God to help him with the things God has given him a wife to help him with. In other words, some men are guilty of calling everyone for assistance before talking to the one person God Himself defined as their help.

Then, when things go badly, the only person standing with the man is the GREAT WOMAN. The Help Meet was not given to man to be dominated or subjugated as a sexual slave, nor is she given to him to be abused, but to help him to be fruitful and multiply. She was given to him to help him to have dominion in the earth. That, my precious reader, was God's plan for marriage from the beginning. When sin entered the picture, everything was perverted including the way men treated their Help Meet. I am not implying that all men dominate and subjugate women, but what I am saying is this: sin is in every man, and with it comes the propensity and the proclivity for abuse. The New Man in Christ is not just a moral being because there are many people who are moral and have no fellowship with Christ. In Christ, the New Man has a new nature, a nature that is not sin laden and sin dominated.

I was not saved when I married, so I came to the marriage with a lot of BAGGAGE. I was born into a Jamaican culture that was and is very macho and patriarchal. I had to unlearn a lot of things, and be delivered from a chauvinistic mindset and thought process which manifested in bad habits, so I could know how to treat the treasure, the gift, the Help Meet given to me by Father God in the form of a wife. There is nothing wrong with being single. According to Dr. Monica Hardy, author of Embracing God: My Season of Single, never underestimate the value of a season. When single, take advantage of your alone season with God. Whereas, God had to separate Himself, it was for a defined purpose and only a season. Throughout scripture we find that Jesus often separated Himself to be alone to hear from our Heavenly Father—this process is called sanctification. God gives some individuals the grace to live in such a state (some are even gifted with celibacy), but for the majority, the plan of God is that a man should have a wife as a Help Meet, and a companion. Irrespective of the laws men pass, that wife is meant to be a woman, and that means a man cannot be another man's wife. The WOMAN was created from man's rib, from his side, to be by his side as he executed the divine assignment given to Him by his Creator God!

MY RIB

"And the Lord God caused a deep sleep to fall upon Adam and he slept: and he took one of his ribs, and closed up the flesh instead thereof;

And the rib, which the Lord God had taken from man, made he a woman, and brought her unto the man" (Genesis 2:21-22). In Dr. Myles Munroe's book, Understanding the Purpose and Power of Woman, he so carefully articulated that God did not create the woman as an afterthought, but as an integral part of His plan in creation. According to Dr. Munroe the female is unique in five significant ways (Munroe, 2001):

1. A woman is God's idea
2. A woman has a spirit inside
3. A woman was taken out of man
4. A woman is physically different from man
5. A woman was specifically placed in the Garden of Eden by God along with man

In other words, the woman was God's idea, so I concur with what Dr. Monica wrote in the foreword for this book: "a man cannot say what a woman can or cannot do, or what a woman is capable of, because he was asleep when she was created." Almighty God does not do anything by accident. I've always wondered why He chose a rib when creating the first woman. Finally, I decided to look up the purpose of the ribs. As per the online site, reference.com, the ribs have three important functions: support, respiration and protection. The ribs protect the heart, liver, kidneys and the lungs from any external injury. The ribs assist in breathing. So! Support, breathing, and protection; now I see why God chose the rib as the starting point for creating the woman. The woman is a great support, she is like a breath of fresh air, and she will give all she has to protect her family. In the Jamieson, Fausset & Brown Commentary Critical and Explanatory on the whole Bible, Robert Jamieson wrote: "She was not made out of his head to surpass him, nor from his feet to be trampled on, but from his side to be equal to him and near his heart to be dear to him."

Second to salvation, which leads to eternal life with God, His greatest gift to man is, WOMAN. The Bible describes children as a heritage; grandchildren are called the crown of old men, but we could not get this type of heritage and crown without the womb of the woman. Her role in life is so important that in His infinite wisdom, Father God shows her importance by not exempting her from the process of bringing His only begotten Son into the world. In His Sovereignty, He chose not to use a man to be Jesus' biological father, but He shows the importance of the woman by using her womb to conceive, nurture and birth His Son. I call women, The Crowning Jewels of God's Creation!

LEAVE AND CLEAVE

"And Adam said, This is now bone of my bones, and flesh of my flesh: she shall be called Woman, because she was taken out of Man. Therefore shall a man leave his father and his mother, and shall cleave unto his wife: and they shall be one flesh" (Genesis 2:23-24).

Eve was such a beautiful and precious being, and Adam was so astonished that when he saw her he said, WO—MAN! Adam saw another side of himself when he saw Eve, a side of himself that could help him pro-create and be fruitful. When a man abuses his wife, it is akin to self-abuse because the two are one. Every man should look at his wife or wife-to-be as a gift from God, an extension of himself who is there to help him be who God has created Him to be. I remember speaking to my sister, Janet, about family and she told me: "your wife and children are your family and the people you are related to are your relatives." When she blessed me with that nugget of information, I started to realize what the Lord meant when He said, "leave and cleave." As a man, I had to be grateful for the things I learned from my parents, but once I married I had to leave my father and mother and cleave to my wife so we could become one.

You have some Momma's Boys out there who get married, but cannot cleave to their wives because momma is in the middle. With momma in the middle you have three and not two. Some men leave father and mother, but find it difficult to cleave to their wives because they stay connected to another person or thing which causes a hindrance. My mother is the very first Great Woman in my life. Without her I would fail to exist. My mother instilled priceless values, ethics, standards and principles in my life; she became even greater when she embraced the transition I had to make from son of Monica to husband of Paulette.

MY GOOD THING

As I reflect, I married Paulette at the tender age of twenty-four. I must admit, at that time I knew very little about being a husband, let alone a great husband. Every married couple will tell you the honeymoon does not last forever; it takes hard work and great sacrifice to build a successful marriage. Many couples have tried and failed, but it was not until I submitted to the Lordship of Jesus Christ in prison and read His word, that I realized what the Bible says about a wife.

"Whoso findeth a wife findeth a good thing, and obtaineth favour of the Lord" (Proverbs 18:22). When God saved me and opened my eyes, I started learning and I am still learning what life is all about from His word. I learned God's instructions and expectation of me as a husband. I gleaned wisdom from, 1 Peter 3:7: "Likewise, ye husbands, dwell with them according to knowledge, giving honour unto the wife, as unto the weaker vessel, and as being heirs together of the grace of life; that your prayers be not hindered." Weaker should not be mistaken for inferior; likewise, physically weaker in the flesh or body, does not mean spiritually weaker or weaker in the Kingdom of God. There are times when I look at Paulette and tears come to my eyes. Not tears of sorrow, but tears of joy for being blessed by the Lord with a Great Woman, who is my wife for life! I learned to appreciate my Good Thing; my Help Meet; my Rib; the Wife He allowed me to find. I thank Him for the favor, the answered prayers I have obtained by finding her and treating her according to His instructions. I have not been a perfect husband by any measure, but I am currently celebrating thirty years of marriage to Paulette because of my willingness to submit my human imperfections to God, my willingness to stay in a posture of learning, so I can mature as a husband!

DISTINCT QUALITIES OF GREATNESS

- Meek and Humble Spirit
- Able to Endure Intense Heat and Pressure
- Committed to Prayer
- Hold Household Together
- Faith
- Long Suffering
- Voice of Wisdom and Reason
- Able to Multi-task
- Possess Love and Patience

Naomi

Refuse to Be Bitter: It Was Sent to Make You Better

NAOMI—RESILIENCE PERSONIFIED

really strong woman accepts the war she went through and is ennobled by her scars. —Carly Simon

The majority of messages I've heard taught, or preached from the book of Ruth, revolved around Ruth finding her Boaz. I've heard many single women use the expression, "I'm waiting for my Boaz." The book of Ruth encompasses so much more than singleness and praying for holy matrimony. It details the story of two Great Women of the Bible who epitomize great resilience and fortitude. These great women had an inner strength that allowed them to triumph over immense tragedy. This is a story of a mother and her daughter-in-law who was dedicated and devoted to her. Mothers- in-law often get a bad rap. I once heard a joke which stated, "Behind every successful man there is a…" he paused for a few seconds so the audience could say; a good woman, then he said "NO, an angry mother in-law." However, Naomi was not an angry mother-in-law; on the contrary, she was and is a model for every mother in-law.

Naomi's name means lovable or my delight. She lived at a time when the judges ruled Israel and it was a very turbulent time. The great leader Moses and his minister and successor Joshua were gone and the people rebelled against God. When they rebelled, God allowed their enemies to conquer them. Whenever they repented God raised up a judge to lead them in victory against their enemy, then they would repeat the cycle all over. During that time and season, three Great Women came to the forefront: Deborah, Ruth and Naomi. Each of these women exuded strength and great resolve.

Naomi and her family lived in Bethlehem–Judah, but had to sojourn in the country of Moab, because a devastating famine hit the land. In their book, Women of the Bible, Ann Spangler and Jean E. Syswerda wrote: "There are two rainy seasons in Palestine—October-November and March-April. When rain didn't fall during these two periods, famine resulted. Famine could also occur when hail or insects destroyed the food supply or when invading armies devastated crops in order to bring a captured people into submission.

Throughout scripture God seemed to use famine to bring about His purposes" (133). Naomi, her husband, Elimelech, and their two sons left their hometown of Bethlehem-Judah and went to sojourn in the country of Moab when there was a famine in Israel. Three key words I want you to take note of: Famine, Bethlehem-Judah and Moab: Words that should not be together in the same sentence. WHY? Bethlehem-Judah means house of bread-praise. When connected to the house of bread and praise there should not be a famine in your life, except when there is rebellion against God.

TESTIMONY

The Lord spoke to my heart and instructed me to spend more time reading, studying His word, praying, fasting and worshipping Him. Those instructions meant I had to cut back on my ministry travel schedule. Bills do not step back because you cut back. I had to trust God's providing hand during the season of stillness in His presence. Once I obeyed, God manifested Himself as Jehovah Jireh, my provider. I received a message from one of the Prophetic Destiny Impact Callers, a Great Woman of God who prays constantly and spends countless hours serving and blessing people. She sent me a message and in it she released a prophetic word into my life: "I know thy works: behold, I have set before thee an open door, and no man can shut it. You will see the opportunities I will lay before you today. You will see every ministry opportunity, every business opportunity, and opportunities for financial increase. You will not miss it by being distracted or caught up in the cares of life. You will see clearly what I set before you and you will seize it; says the Lord." A little after twelve that same day, my wife handed me an envelope that came in the mail and in it there was a check for $150.00. When I checked my text messages I saw one that came in the day before which read, "Apostle, I just sent you a seed via PayPal." When I checked PayPal the seed was for $500.00. Even when you are on the battlefield doing the will of God, if God redirects you, He will still make sure your needs are met if you are obedient. Because of the famine, Elimelech and his family went to sojourn in the country of Moab. The word Moab means seed of my father and unfortunately, that seed was not good. Moab and his brother Amon, from which these nations came, were by products of Lot's drunken, incestuous escapades with his daughters.

Naomi

The conditions in Bethlehem-Judah must have been terrible for the man of God to move his family to Moab. It was not the ideal place for them to dwell when they left their home, but when God has a plan for your life He will find you wherever you are dwelling. There are times and seasons in your life when things appear to get worse before they get better; that was the case with Naomi and Ruth. It is in those times when you must resolve to be strong and trust God. It is in those times when you have to rebuff the encroachment of demonically inspired voices that attempt to shipwreck your faith. Naomi dwelled in Moab for ten years and three things happened to greatly test her resolve.

1) Her husband died leaving her a widow
2) Her sons took Moabitess women for their wives
3) Her two sons later died in Moab

The death of a child or children is one of the greatest griefs a woman can suffer. It is important to understand how difficult life was for women of that day who had no husbands or sons. 2 Kings 4:1 says: "Now there cried a certain woman of the wives of the sons of the prophets unto Elisha, saying, Thy servant my husband is dead; and thou knowest that thy servant did fear the Lord: and the creditor is come to take unto him my two sons to be bondmen." In those times families did back breaking work in farming and raising livestock, so a woman who did not have a husband or sons was in dire straits. Unlike the widow who came to Elisha for help, Naomi had no male help.

When faced with adversity, there are two choices: be deterred or be determined. Adversity can destroy or build character and Naomi chose the latter of each, which is why she is in my hall of faith for great women. She had her moments of weakness as all of us would when hit with such a life changing tragedy as the loss of a beloved husband and two loving sons. Many fail to realize that every loss must be grieved, but what do you do when you have a triple loss all at once? The loss of a child has to be one of the most difficult things any parent will deal with, especially a mother who carried that child in her womb and nurtured him or her. However, Naomi had the tenacity to thrive and survive.

RISE, SHINE AND GIVE GOD THE GLORY

Here is something worth paying close attention to; Naomi's great fortitude started to manifest when her sons Mahlon and Chilion died. The Bible declares: "then she arose with her daughters-in-law." I love the language here; she was devastated by the great loss, but she did not allow it to bury her in deep depression. She arose and took her sons' wives with her. The fact that her daughters-in-law were widows also must be mentioned. Not only did she have to be strong for herself, she also had to be strong for them. She may not have been happy that her sons married Moabite women, because of the instructions given to Moses by God, but she grew to love them. God's instructions to Moses were: "An Ammonite or Moabite shall not enter into the congregation of the Lord; even to their tenth generation shall they not enter into the congregation of the Lord forever: Because they met you not with bread and with water in the way, when ye came forth out of Egypt; and because they hired against thee Balaam the son of Beor of Pethor of Mesopotamia, to curse thee" (Deuteronomy 23:3-4). God is merciful, He is loving and He is kind. Naomi does not appear to hold any prejudice against the wives of her sons; she showed them love. Many marriages have been destroyed because momma refused to stop meddling when her son married a woman she did not approve of. Naomi did not wallow in misery and pity; she arose. Like Naomi, arise and get ready to soar like the great eagle you were created to be. Refuse to throw in the towel, refuse to waive the white flag of surrender, for forward is still Jehovah's will. When the adversary is looking to attend your pity party he has to flee. When he shows up expecting pity make sure he hears your praise!

When you arise you must have a plan and know your purpose. If you don't know where you are going, any road will lead you there. Naomi arose with her daughters-in-law that she might return from the country of Moab. Whatever or wherever your Moab is, never stop looking for an exit. You may have lost some people or things that were near and dear to you when you were in Moab, but restoration is coming if you are willing to arise. When Job lost all his children, all his wealth and his health—his body was in pain because of the boils that covered him from head to toe—he still believed God and was steadfast in his belief that God would keep him.

To further test his will, his wife even asked, "Dost thou still retain thine integrity? Curse God, and die."

However, Job referenced her as a foolish woman and not a great woman. Beloved, whatever you have lost in Moab, whether it is your marriage, a child, a spouse or your freedom, refuse to lose your integrity; do not allow the enemy to talk you out of it. I have witnessed many Great Women up close and personal go through major tragedies, but Great Women maintain their integrity in the midst of their struggle no matter how great the tragedy.

My friend and sister in the Lord, Cynthia Smith, worked and kept the household together while her husband was hospitalized for two months due to a fall on his job, eventually becoming unresponsive due to a stroke. He was in rehab for two and a half years and yet, she maintained a constant vigil at his bedside and was strong for herself and their four children until he went home to be with the Lord. As you can see, Moab will test your mettle and it will challenge your faith, but Great Women will rise to the occasion every time.

FAITH COMES BY HEARING

The catalyst that caused Naomi to arise was what she heard in the country of Moab—how the Lord had visited His people and provided them with bread during a time of famine. Naomi refused to allow the immensity of her tragedy to impair her hearing by causing her ear gate to wax full of doubt and fear. Faith comes by hearing and hearing by the word; so when you allow the tragedy to speak louder than your ability to hear God, you allow it to negatively affect your faith.

She was already dealing with a heavy heart because of the loss of her husband and her sons, but she kept her ear gate in tuned to what the Lord was saying. If you compare Naomi's response to that of Job's wife, both women dealt with great loss. Naomi heard what the Lord was doing and simply got up. When things get really bad it is easy to give up. Job's wife looked at the state of her husband and talked about cursing God and dying. Be careful what you allow to come out of your mouth when dealing with a Moab tragedy. There are some folks around you who are amazed that you are still giving God glory in spite of all you have gone and are going through. They do not understand the depth of your relationship with Him. Since Moab represents a strange place or situation you find yourself in, what or where is your Moab and what are you hearing and doing in the midst of your Moab? Remember, Naomi heard what the Lord was doing in the midst of His people and she arose.

Beloved, a move of God is always precipitated and accompanied by a sound, so if you cannot hear the sound you will miss the move. "Blessed is the people that know the joyful sound: they shall walk, O Lord, in the light of thy countenance" (Psalms 89:15). No matter how difficult your affliction, keep your ears calibrated to the sound of heaven. In Isaiah 6, the prophet saw the great vision of the Lord seated on His throne. In describing the seraphims—the prophet declared, "And one cried unto another, and said, Holy, holy, holy, is the Lord of hosts; the whole earth is full of his glory. And the posts of the door moved at the voice of him that cried, and the house was filled with smoke." As indicated in the text, there was a sound and then there was movement. Smoke represented the glory. In other words, you are the house and Christ is in you. While the religious chickens are running all over the place trying to get a word and trying to get a move, you are an Eagle that knows how to make a sound in prayer and a sound in praise that will cause the Glory to rise and fill the house. Paul and Silas made a powerful sound through praise that caused a move of God that shook the very foundations of the prison causing the doors to be opened.

"And when the day of Pentecost was fully come, they were all with one accord in one place. And suddenly there came a sound from heaven as of a rushing mighty wind, and it filled all the house where they were sitting. And there appeared unto them cloven tongues like as of fire, and it sat upon each of them."(Acts 2:1-3) That sound from heaven started the New Testament Church and three thousand souls were added that day. It was the sound of prayer that precipitated the move of God that ushered in the Azusa Street Revival. Whatever or wherever the strange place is, it is time for you to go forth out of that place and get back to Judah, the place of praise and the visitation of the Lord. Depart from Moab and get back to Judah!

DISTINCT QUALITIES OF GREATNESS

- Generous
- Not Afraid to Show Her She-motions
- Able to Rise Above Tragic Situations
- Discerning Ears to Hear What the Lord is Doing
- Unwavering Faith
- Mentor
- Able to Facilitate and Help Others to Reach Their Destiny
- Wise Counselor
- Nurturer

Ruth

A Winner Never Quits, and a Quitter Never Wins

RUTH—STEADFAST COMMITMENT

strong Woman knows she has strength enough for the journey, but a Woman of Strength knows it is in the journey where she will become strong. —www.feelmylove.org

The lives of Naomi and Ruth are so connected that Ruth's story has to follow Naomi's for the purpose of continuity. As previously stated, the story of Ruth is always told in relation not only to Naomi, but her connection to Boaz the kinsman redeemer. However, before she ever met Boaz, she had some attributes that qualified her to wear the mantle of a Great Woman. You may not come from a wealthy or educated family or you may have married into a family with varied issues, but if you have the attributes like Ruth, God can and will bring greatness out of your life. Of all the people in the world who have come and gone, Ruth does not only have her story in the Bible, but a book of the Bible in her name. God chose you before the foundation of the world to make an impact for His kingdom so your name is written in heaven.

DON'T LEAVE—CLEAVE

Husbands are instructed in the word of God to leave and cleave, but Ruth decided to cleave and never leave. "And Naomi said unto her two daughters-in-law, Go, return each to her mother's house: the LORD deal kindly with you, as ye have dealt with the dead and with me" (Ruth 1:8). This passage informs us that both women were kind to their husbands and they were kind to Naomi. She pronounced a blessing over them when she declared: "The LORD grant you that ye may find rest, each of you in the house of her husband. Then she kissed them; and they lifted up their voice, and wept" (Ruth 1:9). The daughters-in-law insisted Naomi take them with her, but she encouraged them to go back to their mothers' house because she was not able to give them husbands. They lifted up their voices and wept again; Orpah kissed her mother in law; but Ruth showed her greatness when she clave unto her (Ruth 1:14). Ruth made up her mind to stay; she was not going to leave Naomi no matter the consequences. The Hebrew word for cleave is: dabaq, pronounced, (daw-bak'); it means, to cling or adhere; to catch by pursuit: follow close (hard after), be joined together, overtake, pursue hard.

It is interesting to note the name Ruth is derived from the Hebrew word (re'ut) meaning friend. The Bible states, "there is a friend that sticketh closer than a brother" (Proverbs 18:24b). However, Orpah means fawn, which is a young deer, especially an un-weaned one - that speaks of immaturity. Unlike Orpah, Ruth was willing to leave her comfort zone, her land and her kindred. Although Ruth was dealing with her own tragic loss (she had been widowed like Naomi) she still found the strength, courage and fortitude to serve and strengthen her mother-in-law. The true sign of maturity and greatness is the willingness and ability to stand with others while you are dealing with a crisis, knowing Christ is with you in the crisis.

DON'T RETREAT—ENTREAT

Naomi told Ruth that her sister-in-law had gone back to her people and back to her gods and she should do the same, but Ruth would have none of it because Great Women are pioneers, trailblazers and trendsetters. "And Ruth said, entreat me not to leave thee, or to return from following after thee: for whither thou goest, I will go; and where thou lodgest, I will lodge: thy people shall be my people, and thy God my God: Where thou diest, will I die, and there will I be buried: the Lord do so to me, and more also, if ought but death part thee and me. When she saw that she was steadfastly minded to go with her, then she left speaking unto her" (Ruth 1:16-18). Ruth's response to Naomi is one of the greatest responses you can hear as it encapsulates greatness. The Hebrew word for steadfastly is 'amats', pronounced, (aw-mats'); it means, to be alert, physically (on foot) or mentally (in courage): confirm, be courageous (of good courage) to fortify, harden, increase, prevail, strengthen (self). Upon Naomi's return to her hometown (Bethlehem of Judah), the response of the people exemplified how the tragic loss of her husband and sons had affected her and how valuable and needed Ruth's support was. The people asked, "Is this Naomi?" Ten long years in Moab and some tragic losses made her almost unrecognizable. "And she said unto them, call me not Naomi, call me Mara: for the Almighty hath dealt very bitterly with me. I went out full, and the Lord hath brought me home again empty: why then call ye me Naomi, seeing the Lord hath testified against me, and the Almighty hath afflicted me" (Ruth 1:20-21)?

Out of the abundance of the heart the mouth speaks. Naomi's words revealed how heavy her heart was, but God was not finished with her.

She did not know it at the time, but God had a great plan and she was right in the middle of it. You may not be able to discern the plan of God when you are dealing with your tragedy, but keep your faith and your praise intact because the greater plan of God will be revealed to you and through you. The name Naomi means lovable or my delight, but Mara means bitterness. Marah was a fountain at the sixth station of the Israelites (Exodus 15:23-24; Numbers 33:8) whose waters were so bitter that they could not drink them. The number six represents self; it is not a coincidence that at the sixth station the waters were bitter. On this account they murmured against Moses, who, under divine direction, cast into the fountain "a certain tree" which took away its bitterness, so that the people drank of it. Jesus is the tree of eternal life; He makes the bitter waters sweet. "In the last day, that great day of the feast, Jesus stood and cried, saying, if any man thirst, let him come unto me, and drink. He that believeth on me, as the scripture hath said, out of his belly shall flow rivers of living water" (John 7:37-38). Ruth had to rise above her own mourning to keep Naomi encouraged. She discerned the condition of Naomi and refused to let her return to Bethlehem by herself. When you are leaving Moab, you need someone who will go with you, come what may.

Naomi left during a famine, but God is so strategic that He allowed her and Ruth to return at the beginning of the Barley Harvest. The Barley Harvest manifests during the spring when things are growing and fruitful. For those of you that have been faithful in your commitment to serve and you have blessed others while dealing with your own tragedy. God is going to shift you to a place where the harvest is just beginning! Whenever there is a shift, God will place the people or resources you need all around you. He is a very present help in the time of trouble and He always has a ram in the thicket. Ruth was a stranger in Bethlehem and Naomi had been gone for ten years so they needed help since the males in their lives were deceased. God never leaves nor forsakes a widow. God used Boaz, the kinsman redeemer, to bless them. Boaz means alacrity, which means cheerful readiness, promptness and willingness. The Bible states, "And Naomi had a kinsman of her husband's, a mighty man of wealth, of the family of Elimelech; and his name was Boaz" (Ruth 2:1). God is the only one who can cause you to triumph greatly over tragedy. Elimelech and their sons were gone, but God had a Boaz in the wings who would take them to the next dimension. If you have experienced a famine or have suffered great loss, Jesus Christ is your Kinsman Redeemer, the only one anointed to bless and prosper you. "And Ruth, the Moabitess, said unto Naomi, let me now go to the field, and glean ears of corn after him in whose sight I shall find grace. And she said unto her, Go, my daughter" (Ruth 2:2).

When Boaz saw Ruth, he asked his servants who the damsel was and they told him she was the Moabitess who had returned with Naomi out of the land of Moab. Listen, Great Women, when you are faithful over the little, God will make sure you are recognized by someone of great wealth and stature. So, wait on your Boaz. Don't settle for Bozo or a Jack-az. Someone put a post on YouTube which said it best; if you are not careful, you will hook up with a…

Broke-az
Po-az
Lyin-az
Cheatin-az
Dumb-az
Drunk-az
Lockedup-az
Lazy-az
Good-for-nothing-az
Beatinyo-az

Most importantly, make sure he respects Yo-az!

In her book, Embracing God: My Season of Single, Dr. Hardy clarifies what it means to settle. She said, SETTLING is what happens when you see the forest and not the trees. You see leaves and branches and think it is a tree when in actuality it is the clutter and woodiness of the forest. In other words, settling is accepting less because you feel you cannot do better or you don't want to wait on God to send better. Moreover, settling also means coming to resolve, and at some point, we all must come to resolve. Make sure you have identified your non-negotiable priorities because those are not to be compromised. So yes, you do have to settle on a decision, but you are not settling for less (Hardy, 2017). As you can see, Ruth did not settle; she was strategic. She asked and received permission from Boaz to glean in his field. In other words, she positioned herself for observation in preparation for manifestation. "And Boaz answered and said unto her, It hath fully been shewed me, all that thou hast done unto thy mother-in-law since the death of thine husband: and how thou hast left thy father and thy mother, and the land of thy nativity, and art come unto a people which thou knewest not heretofore. The Lord recompense thy work, and a full reward be given thee of the Lord God of Israel, under whose wings thou art come to trust" (Ruth 2:11-12).

Boaz heard about Ruth. He received the full dossier on Ruth from the time she was in Moab serving her mother-in-law. Ruth's purpose for leaving Moab was not to find her Boaz, but He found her in her serving. Serving faithfully is key. You never know whose ears your unselfish deeds towards another are reaching. Don't serve to be found, but be found serving. Keep serving without looking for recognition or people to call your name or pat you on the back. Jesus, the Kinsman Redeemer, knows your labor of love and will recompense you with a full reward; He is not going to give you a partial blessing. David declared, "Thou anointest my head with oil, my cup runnneth over"(Psalms 23:5b). God anoints the head of the faithful with the oil of joy. He causes their cups to overflow. It may seem like a long time coming, but God never forgets. Do not faint or become weary in well doing; in your due season you will reap like the Great Woman, Ruth.

Boaz married Ruth; my Kingdom colleague Dr. Hardy stated, "I need a man who is going to do life WITH me." In essence, she wants someone willing to travel or take the journey with her. Boaz was there for all aspects of Ruth's life: the highs and lows, the ebbs and flows. Thus, Ruth conceived and birthed a son whom the women, her neighbors, named Obed, who is the father of Jessie, the father of David. "And the women said unto Naomi, blessed be the Lord, which hath not left thee this day without a kinsman, that his name may be famous in Israel. And he shall be unto thee a restorer of thy life, and a nourisher of thine old age: for thy daughter-in-law, which loveth thee, which is better to thee than seven sons, hath borne him. And Naomi took the child, and laid it in her bosom, and became nurse unto it" (Ruth 4:14-16). What a beautiful picture of restoration. Naomi and Ruth persevered through the pain of their respective tragedies. Ruth followed her mother-in-law Naomi back to her hometown and, through divine providence, the Lord connected her to Boaz who gave Naomi a male seed through Ruth. That male seed started a lineage that produced the greatest seed of all, the seed of Mary who would bruise the head of the serpent; that seed is Jesus Christ the Savior of the world. The connection of Ruth and Boaz is fascinating because she is a Moabitess and he is a descendant of Rahab who was a harlot. Truly, God is no respecter of persons. Where are the Ruths who are willing to keep their flesh in check and serve faithfully? Great woman you are a good thing waiting to be found so keep serving, keep caring, keep loving. The receiver of your favor is on the way.

DISTINCT QUALITIES OF GREATNESS

- Generosity
- Humility
- Loyalty
- Loving
- Strength
- Encouraging
- Willingness to Leave Comfort Zone for New Horizons
- Willingness to Go Forward When Others Turn Back
- Submission to Godly Authority

Section Two

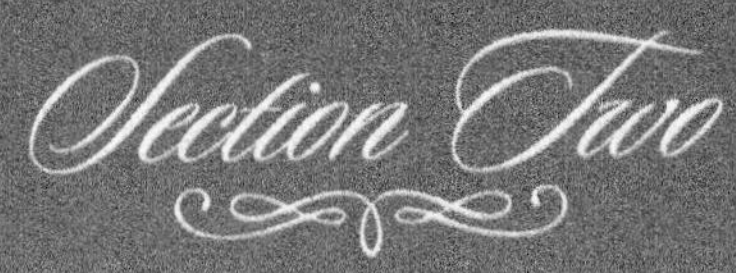

PIONEERS, TRAILBLAZERS & TRENDSETTERS

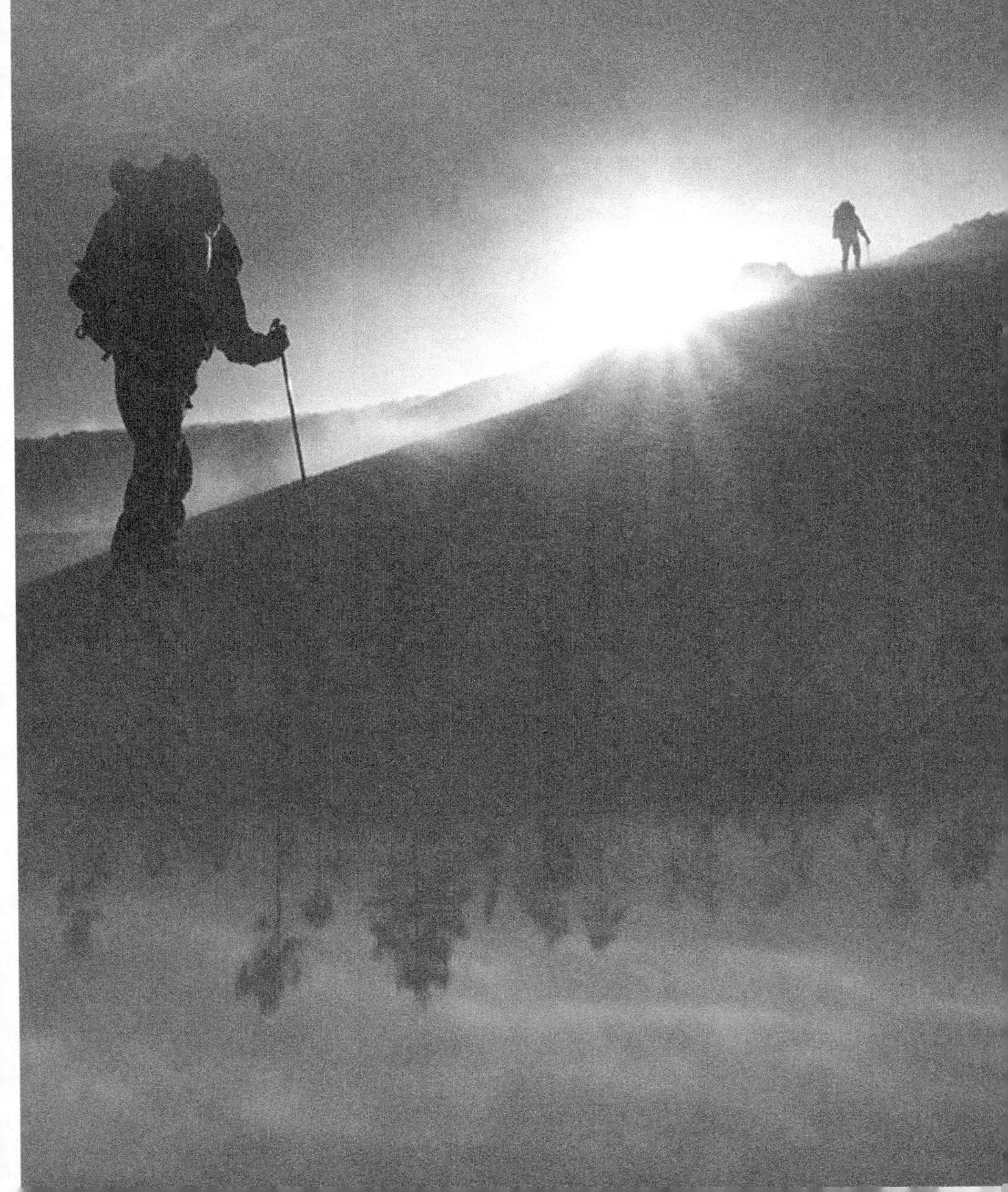

The Daughters of Zelophehad

Team Work Makes the Dream Work

THE DAUGHTERS OF ZELOPHEHAD—PARADIGM SHIFTERS

*how me your company and I'll tell you who you are. —My Mom, Monica Donaldson*

The Bible truly is the living word of God. You can read it time and time again, and at any given moment the Holy Spirit will illuminate the word in a manner you have not previously seen. I have read the story of the Daughters of Zelophehad on many occasions, but one day a good friend and kingdom colleague, Pastor Eileen Chatman, made reference to them in a conversation with such passion, that I felt the resonance in my soul to study them further.

In the book of Numbers 27:7, you will find the Daughters of Zelophehad. Those ladies were descendants of Manasseh who was the first son of Joseph. They were five sisters who refused to settle for the status quo in Israel and that refusal caused them to take action, which resulted in a global paradigm shift. These sisters lived at a time when Israel was about to enter the Promised Land. Their father was deceased and according to the Mosaic laws, a father's inheritance went to his son or sons once he died. Their father, Zelophehad, died and did not have any male heirs, only his five daughters. What was to be done with the inheritance that he left behind? According to Barnes' Notes on the Bible in biblehub.com— "Women in Israel had not, up to the present time, enjoyed any distinct right of inheritance. Yet a father, whether sons had been born to him or not, had the power, either before or at his death, to cause part of his estate to pass to a daughter."

Unfortunately for Zelophehad's daughters, he did not leave instructions for them to inherit land but these sisters took initiative. When they heard the land was to be divided among those that were numbered, males twenty years or older, they became concerned they would have no share in the land since their father was dead and there were no sons. Per the commentary from Cambridge Bible for Schools and Colleges (biblehub.com):

"The incident here related is regarded as an historical occurrence in the life of individuals. Its purpose is to introduce the law of inheritance." The commentary in Cambridge Bible for Schools and Colleges further states: "The Hebrews always adhered firmly to the principle that landed property must not be alienated from the tribe or family to which it belonged." In early days, inheritance by daughters was not contemplated. If a man died without children, his widow should be married to his brother in order to bear sons who would inherit the property.

The five sisters refused to lower their standards, compromise their integrity, or sit idly by while the land was about to be allotted to someone else based on gender. Mahlah, Noah, Hoglah, Milcah, and Tirzah stood before Moses and before Eleazar the priest. These women did not create a box so they would not have to step out of one; in this patriarchal society, they refused to 'know their place' because they knew their place. They wanted their inheritance; they wanted what was rightly theirs and they made a bold move in approaching Moses to get it. Moses and Eleazar were not the only ones there. The princes and the congregation were at the meeting place, which was by the door of the tabernacle. This could not have been an easy thing to do because that culture and society was male dominated. At the time of the writing of this manuscript—in Saudi Arabia, there is a guardianship system, which prevents women from doing vital tasks without getting permission from a male relative. They are unable to obtain a passport or travel abroad without the consent of their husband, father or another male relative.

The Daughters of Zelophehad told Moses that their father had died in the wilderness, but he was not among those who gathered themselves against the Lord in the rebellion of Korah. They made their case succinctly and in an articulate manner. They explained to Moses that their father died without sons so they challenged Moses by asking, "Why should the name of our father be done away from among his family, because he hath no son?" (Numbers 27:4). This question provoked thought and after questioning Moses, those Great Women shifted and made a bold, emphatic statement, "Give unto us therefore a possession among the brethren of our father!"

The Daughters of Zelophehad

POSSESSING YOUR POSSESSION!

Great women, do not allow your gender, ethnicity, lack of education or anything else to hinder you from possessing the inheritance that your Father in heaven has for you. In the culture of the Old Testament, the son was first in line for the inheritance left from a deceased father's estate, but in the kingdom, God sent His only begotten Son to die so everyone in His family can have an inheritance—irrespective of gender, ethnicity, class or color. He gave us a New Testament, a New Will and a New Covenant, which tells us of all the blessings we will inherit in earth and in heaven. Do not allow man-made glass ceilings to block your elevation and promotion. Do not allow them to stifle your creativity and suppress the greatness that you have inherited from your heavenly Father's DNA.

We came out of our mothers' wombs as sons and daughters, but in the Kingdom we are all sons of God in Jesus Christ. In the kingdom, greatness is not based on gender but on our submission to the will of our Father in heaven. Our daughters must know they have greatness dwelling inside them, and they must endeavor to do what is necessary to allow that greatness to come forth. I cannot understand societies where females are not allowed to get an education. I was shocked when I heard that the Taliban banned girls from going to school. Girls in Afghanistan have had acid thrown in their faces because they went to school. In another horrific event, 160 girls at an Afghan school were poisoned. From the day the serpent entered the garden, there has been an attack against women by demonic forces trying to hinder their greatness. Since men and women together make one, men must see these attacks against women as an attack against themselves. Instead of joining in these demonic attacks against the female gender, we as men should fight the enemy that is after our women. In no way should we join forces with the devil against our mothers, sisters, wives and daughters.

The Daughters of Zelophehad's presentation of their case to Moses was so well put together that Moses brought their case before the Lord. I wonder how many men have allowed chauvinistic, misogynistic biases to deafen their ears and callous their hearts when a woman presented her request before them? Moses was a true Man of God who was led by the Spirit and not bound by legalistic traditions and cultural norms. He was meek and humble enough to not decide on their request without consulting the Lord.

We need more leaders like Moses who will not see a situation through lens tainted by gender or any other form of bias. We need great women like the Daughters of Zelophehad who are not afraid or intimidated, but willing to step out of their place of comfort and be pioneers, trailblazers and trendsetters.

The Lord responded positively to Moses and said, "The daughters of Zelophehad speak right" (Numbers 27:7). What a day of rejoicing that must have been—not only for them, but for all the women in Israel as a precedence was being set. That is why Great Women are women who know how to take initiative; they know how to make their case. They do not sit around lamenting a situation waiting and hoping for change to come; they step up and they step out to become initiators of change, to be paradigm shifters. The Lord told Moses, "thou shalt surely give them a possession of an inheritance among their father's brethren; and thou shalt cause the inheritance of their father to pass unto them." When God says something, it is etched in something greater than stone, it is settled in eternity. Always remember, if you do not ask, then the answer will be no, but if you open your mouth and let your request be known you have a good chance of having your request granted. The Daughters of Zelophehad were not going to be without an inheritance in the Promised Land. In Numbers 27:8, God spoke to Moses and set an ordinance in the nation: "Thou shalt speak unto the children of Israel, saying, if a man die, and have no son, then ye shall cause his inheritance to pass unto his daughter."

DISTINCT QUALITIES OF GREATNESS

- Refuse to Settle for the Status Quo
- Take Action
- Take the Initiative (be proactive)
- Refuse to Lower Your Standards
- Refuse to Compromise Your Integrity
- Articulate Your Concerns
- Claim What is Rightfully Yours
- Do Not Be Intimidated
- Be a History Maker

Deborah

In the Storm Chickens See Opposition; Eagles See Opportunity

DEBORAH—LEADERSHIP TO LEADER-SHIFT

here was one of two things I had a right to: Liberty or death. If I could not have one, I would take the other. For no man should take me alive. I should fight for liberty as long as my strength lasted.—Harriet Tubman

You know you are a Great Woman when you are chosen by God to sit under your own tree to judge His people. Such was the mandate for the Great Woman, Prophetess Deborah whose name means, 'Honey Bee.' She flowed in a sweet prophetic and leadership grace. The Jamieson, Fausset, and Brown Commentary states: "She was a woman of extraordinary wisdom and piety, instructed in divine knowledge by the Spirit, and accustomed to interpreting the will of God. She acquired an extensive influence, and was held in universal respect, insomuch that she became the animating mind of the government, and discharged all the special duties of a judge—her prophetic judgeship was in the years, 1209-1169." In their book, Women of the Bible, Ann Spangler and Jean E. Syswerda wrote this about Deborah: "Her vision of the world was shaped not by the political situation of her day but by her relationship with God. Though women in the ancient world did not usually become political leaders, Deborah was just the leader Israel needed—a prophetess who heard God and believed him. And whose courage aroused the people, enabling them to throw off foreign oppression."

She was raised up by God at a time when King Jabin degraded and subjugated Israel for twenty years. At that time, the nation's spirit of patriotism seemed crushed. In the midst of the calamity, Deborah roused the people from a lethargic state. Her fame spread far and wide, and the children of Israel came to her with matters that needed to be judged as she sat in her tent under the palm tree between Ramah and Bethel. Ramah is an elevated place and Bethel means house of God. What an awesome place to be postured and positioned, between elevation and the house of God.

In a male dominated culture, she became a mother in Israel. There were very few women who held that title and distinction in the history of the nation.

Let us wrap our minds around the magnitude of the Great Grace the Great Woman Deborah walked in. Besides being a great prophetess and judge, she was a gifted song writer and singer who sang the praises of Almighty God when He caused them to triumph over their enemies.

As I reflect on the Great Woman, Deborah, I realize the position she held in the nation was greater than many of the male leaders chosen by God today. The majority of the Old Testament prophets prophesied at a time when the nation was ruled by a king and was ministered to by a priest of the Lord on behalf of the people. To specify, Samuel operated in a three-fold anointing of prophet, priest and judge. Moses was a prophet and a judge, but his father-in law told him to appoint seventy elders to help him judge the nation so he would not wear himself out. David was a prophet and king, but for many years he was king over Judah before he was elevated to being king over all Israel. Deborah was one of the few individuals who was a prophet and a leader of the nation.

After the death of the judge Ehud, the children of Israel did evil in the sight of the Lord so He allowed Jabin the king of the Canaanites to dominate them. When he oppressed them, they cried out to the Lord because he had 900 chariots of iron, which he used to subjugate the Israelites for 20 years. The Israelites needed a leader who could destroy the yoke Jabin had around their necks and Prophetess Deborah stepped up with power and authority from God.

Deborah's first order of business was to summon Barak from Kadesh to take command of 10,000 men of Zebulun and Naphtali to lead them to Mount Tabor on the Plain of Esdraelon at its north-east end. They were to go into battle against the army of Jabin, which was commanded by Sisera. Deborah was about business. She was such a towering figure of authority that Barak responded to the command by saying, "If thou wilt go with me, then I will go: but if thou wilt not go with me, then I will not go" (Judges 4:8). His response was astounding when you think about the facts; it was God who sent the instructions to him through His Prophetess Deborah. He had 10,000 men at his command to lead into battle, and he would not go unless God's anointed prophetess went with him—that in itself says a great deal about the stature of God's Great Leader, Deborah.

Deborah told Barak, God would draw unto Him Sisera, the captain of Jabin's army, to the river Kishon with his chariots and his multitude, and would deliver him into Barak's hand.

She agreed to go with him, but told him he would not receive honor out of the trip because the Lord would deliver Sisera into the hands of a woman. The woman who received the honor for killing Sisera was a woman by the name of Jael who drove a nail through his temple. With Barak's aid, Prophetess Deborah organized the army, she gave the signal for attack and the Hebrew host launched their attack against the Canaanite army and almost wiped them out completely.

That was a tremendous and memorable day in Israel. Judges 5 records the song of Deborah, which she wrote in grateful commemoration of that great deliverance. This phenomenal woman was a renaissance woman in that she prophesied, sat in a position of power and authority to judge God's people, helped lead the army into battle, and wrote a triumphal song when the enemy was defeated. Deborah was definitely a woman who refused to allow her gender to hinder her from doing great exploits for God. She refused to allow the good old boys network to hinder her from rising to the occasion as God's anointed, His chosen vessel. There is a clarion call going from God, calling modern day Deborahs to come into their rightful place of leadership. This company of Great Women will not be hindered and they will not be denied their high calling in God. I truly believe that company of Great Women is answering the call and is being used by God to bring Great Deliverance!

GLORY OF ZION

A good friend and fellow minister, Charlett Porter, sent me a link for a video from a great ministry called Glory of Zion. Charlett is always sharing with me how the Glory of the Lord manifests in such an awesome way in Glory of Zion. The ministry is under the leadership of the humble anointed Apostle and Prophet, Chuck Pierce. The service she sent was dedicated to the empowerment of women, so I was really excited because I was working on the manuscript for this book about Great Women. I was humbled and excited that I was in the right spiritual vein in terms of what the Holy Spirit was speaking. There was a guest minister at the church, Pastor Denise Goulet. She spoke about a partnership between men and women, and a coming glory and miracles that would be facilitated through that partnership. The partnership of Deborah and Barak secured victory for God's people. After Pastor Goulet ministered, Chuck Pierce, the man of God, stood up, and with a heavy prophetic oil flowing through him, gave the congregation a prophetic word.

He said: "There is a reserve of power inside us. God is about to call His people, especially women, and that power reserve will manifest through them." This is an explosion of power in God's women that will cause the enemy of the King to flee. "I say to you like I said to Rahab, make a way for many to go into their promise." He told the audience, which was a majority of women, that there was a reserve in them that could activate the reserve in others. "Women get ready; this is a time of new activation, a time of new direction. Go beyond your opinions, go beyond your own desire and come into His desire." He ended by instructing them to give God a shout of victory because His Spirit was there. The company of Great Women Chuck Pierce was prophesying to, are a company of Deborahs who will manifest God's power and authority.

DISTINCT QUALITIES OF GREATNESS

- Leadership Skills and Ability
- Not Afraid to Speak the Word of God with Boldness
- Willing to Go When Others Are Fearful
- Focused
- Extraordinary Wisdom and Piety
- Influence and Respect
- Versatile
- Humble in the Midst of Fame
- Does Not Use Gender as an Excuse for Mediocrity

Esther

Before You Embark on a Journey of Revenge, Dig Two Graves

ESTHER—GOD'S WOMAN ON THE INSIDE

hink like a queen: A queen is not afraid to fail. Failure is another steppingstone to greatness. —Oprah Winfrey

The Sovereignty of God means He is not dependent on anyone or anything in the universe. He raises up some and sits others down. He has mercy on whomsoever He chooses and He avails and advances whomever He wishes. He can use a donkey to speak to a prophet; a rooster to speak to a backslider, money from a fish's mouth to pay taxes, and a raven to feed a prophet. It all presents a perfect picture of the most unlikely of all creatures to secure His divine will upon the earth. God, more often than not, desires to use the ill-equipped, the untrained, the inexperienced, the inept, the disqualified, the disdained, and the most illogical and highly improbable of all candidates such as animals, birds, and beasts of burden who were instrumental in performing His will on the earth.

Throughout the scriptures, God raised up women from a meager existence and humble beginnings and anointed them to be and do great and mighty things. They accomplished extraordinary endeavors despite overwhelming odds. God personally and divinely selected women to impact kingdoms and subdue nations. He elevated and positioned one woman for the preservation of an entire nation and religion: that of God's chosen people. God does not necessarily pursue women possessing great ambition, unlimited fortitude, strong constitution, or dogged determination. On the contrary, He prefers and chooses seemingly fragile, shy, quiet, and unassuming characters. However, once those women shed their natural reticence,the resulting transformation is totally unrecognizable. God is able to supernaturally raise up one in His power, His strength, His knowledge, His courage, and His boldness. He can raise you from a low and dark place into a gilded palace.

One of God's greatest vessels was a young woman, adopted by her cousin and known as Esther, but her Hebrew name was Hadassah, which means Myrtle Tree. The Myrtle Tree has a pleasant fragrance, and Esther's life exuded the aromatic fragrance of God's grace and mercy towards His people. I want to look at Esther's life from the perspective of being strategically positioned by God to impact a nation.

Her life is evidence that no matter how humble your beginnings, God can and will position you in a place to execute His plans.All you have to do is say, "here am I Lord, what would you have me to do?" God is looking for willing and humble vessels to implement His will on the earth in order to fulfill His purposes; not our will as we often want, not man's will which they often demand, but God's will which we often resist. A Jewish minority is living in Persia because of their deportation from Judah. They are facing destruction because of racial hatred, but what the devil's agent does not understand is this: God has created a Great Woman on the inside of Esther that He is going to use to destroy the enemy of His people and save them.

The Bible says Esther was raised by an older cousin, Mordecai, because she had no mother nor father. Although she was an orphan and she was adopted, from the very onset there was evidence of God's divine hand directing her life and ordering her steps. What is the story of your beginning? What is your current state or position? Will you use your adverse circumstances, your wayward upbringing, your grim outlook for the future, your limited resources and abilities, and tragic, haunting experiences as just a shallow excuse to be a mere spectator? Will you hold back and do nothing for God while you continue in a staid, predictable world being static, ordinary, ineffectual, average and mediocre, or will you emerge as an audacious, dynamic, and powerful representative for the Kingdom of God? Will you surrender yourself to the Holy Spirit and willingly allow Him to use your life to display and make God's name known, and reflect His glory?

Will you be a witness for His son Jesus, revolutionizing the universe in spite of a harrowing testimony?

VASHTI—REFUSE TO BE A MAN'S TROPHY

Queen Vashti was deposed by the King when in a drunken state he requested that she parade herself before his courtiers and party guests and she refused- the king therefore sought for a new queen. Some have said that Vashti was rebellious and should have obeyed her husband. I totally disagree. Ahasuerus was a vain king who made a feast in the third year of his reign in an ostentatious effort to display his wealth and the glory of his kingdom. The people who attended his royal parties were given drinks in diverse vessels of gold.

There was a great deal of opulence as the wine flowed, but his ill regard for the queen was very evident, as was the moral decadence in his kingdom. On the seventh day of the party the king's heart was merry with much wine, which means he was inebriated or in simple language, the king was drunk. He ordered seven of his chamberlains to bring Queen Vashti with the royal crown upon her head so the party goers could have the pleasure of gazing upon her beauty. Vashti took a stand and refused to be ogled; she refused to be the object of an ornamental sport and a superficial, beauty trophy. She paid a high price for her disobedience to the king, but that is what Great Women will do to maintain their dignity and respect. Her banishment from the palace led the king on a quest to find a new queen to wear the crown. Little did Ahasuerus know that this was opening the door for the plan of God to be executed.

The royal protocol for selecting a queen was very detailed and meticulous. A group of young maidens was brought to Hegai, the King's chamberlain, and given the oils, incense and spices for their purification. The young women who were virgins, were being prepared so that one could be selected as the new queen. Esther was chosen among the young virgins because she was beautiful and fair to look upon. While man has one plan, God has another. I'm sure Esther was ecstatic at the thought of the once in a life time opportunity to be queen, but God had a much greater plan un be known to her.

Esther found favor in the sight of Hegai the king's chamberlain and keeper of the women, as well as all who looked upon her. When God chooses and positions you, favor will find you. Hegai positioned Esther and her maids into the most favorable place in the house for the women, and immediately provided everything that she needed for her preparation. Any woman who was chosen to go into the king had to go through twelve months of purification consisting of six months with oil of myrrh, and six months with other sweet odors. As was previously stated, Esther means fragrance, and we see such rich typology here as she finds herself in a place of preparation with the sweet scent of the oil of myrrh, and other sweet odors. There is Biblical significance with the numbers twelve and six (months). The number twelve represents Governmental Perfection; Government by Divine Appointment. Six represents flesh, and flesh cannot go into the presence of the king, so the oil of Myrrh is used as a purifying agent to prepare the bride to go into the king. Oil of Myrrh was a principal ingredient in the holy anointing oil (Exodus 30:23).

It was also one of the gifts brought by the wise men from the east, who came to worship the infant Jesus (Matthew 2:11).The church is being prepared as a bride to be betrothed to King Jesus. The Holy Spirit is the oil sent to purify her and to make sure every spot, wrinkle and blemish is removed from her. "Now when the turn of Esther, the daughter of Abihail the uncle of Mordecai, who had taken her for his daughter, was come to go in unto the king, she required nothing but what Hegai the king's chamberlain, the keeper of the women, appointed" (Esther 2:15-17).

God lavished His favor upon Esther and it was precipitous in her being presented before King Ahasuerus in his royal house in the tenth month, in the seventh year of his reign. The tenth month is the month Tebeth, with ten being the number of testimony and seven, the number of completion; a wonderful picture of the testimony of the saints and their perfection in Jesus. The king loved Esther above all the women, and she obtained grace and favor in his sight more than all the virgins. He set the royal crown upon her head, made her queen, and banished Vashti from the palace. Jesus Christ, our Lord and King, had a crown of thorns placed on His head, but is seated at the right hand of majesty with a crown of glory on His head. The grace and favor He gives us will cause us to wear a crown of glory when His perfect work is completed in us.

MUCH MORE THAN A PRETTY FACE

Esther did not obtain favor and elevation to be queen because she had a beautiful, impeccable countenance, or batted her long, silky lashes, or had a come-hither look, or even a seductive manner to capture the heart of the king. No, none of those things mattered in her effort to be crowned queen. God orchestrated things by His divine providence to preserve a posterity for His people. When a wicked racist individual named Haman rose up to destroy the Jews, God was not caught by surprise. His Great Woman, Esther, was favorably positioned inside the palace, not just as another pretty face in the harem, but in a place of authority and influence. Great Women are able to peer deeply beyond the polished veneer and the artificial facade of superficial beauty that goes no further than the skin. They are able to look at the big picture, which is the purpose of their divine positioning. Esther bravely rose to the occasion when she heard that Haman was threatening to destroy the Jews.

Haman an Amelekite, was a descendant of King Agag, an enemy of the Jews. The Amalekites attacked Israel when they came to Rephidim. And now Haman the wicked descendant of Agag was attempting to destroy God's people; what does that tell us? There is an Amalekite spirit that comes through the ages, through generations; it manifested in Hitler when Satan moved him to devise the final solution, his plan to annihilate the Jews. This spirit is alive and well today, infiltrating the hearts of members of the neo-Nazis, Aryan Nations, Ku Klux Klan, Skinheads, and various hate groups who embrace the Spirit of Amalekin regard to the Jewish race, to the Black race, and to other groups with the highest level of scornful contempt. These hate groups have made it their mission to spread their inflammatory, antagonistic message of violent hatred in its most malicious and pernicious forms. We also see it manifesting in the Middle East and other places where Anti-Semitic hatred rears its ugly head. Recently we saw it manifested in the United States of America with Dylann Roof who went into the house of God to commit murder because of racial hate against African Americans. The Lord always has an Esther strategically positioned to thwart the evil plan of the enemy because "There are many plans in a man's heart, but it is God who has the final word" (Proverbs 19:21).

FOR SUCH A TIME AS THIS

Initially Esther did not fully understand her purpose in the palace. This is the response she sent to Mordecai when he sent news to her about the threat from Haman. "All the king's servants, and the people of the king's provinces, do know, that whosoever, whether man or woman, shall come unto the king into the inner court, who is not called, there is one law of his to put him to death, except such to whom the king shall hold out the golden scepter, that he may live: but I have not been called to come in unto the king these thirty days." Thirty represents preparation for the next dimension. Esther was being called to the next dimension, from queen to savior of her people. Although a female, I believe she was a type of Christ in that respect. Types and shadows are not based on gender, but attributes and characteristics. Jesus was adopted by Joseph, Esther was adopted by Mordecai. Jesus is King and Savior, Esther was a queen and a savior for her people. She felt hindered by the palace protocol, but Mordecai's words would stir a spirit of boldness in her, and cause her to fully embrace her calling as God's Great Woman on the Inside. I pray that every woman would have a Mordecai in her life, and not a Haman.

When Mordecai was told of Esther's response, he sent this message to her: "Think not with thyself that thou shalt escape in the king's house, more than all the Jews. For if thou altogether holdest thy peace at this time, then shall there enlargement and deliverance arise to the Jews from another place; but thou and thy father's house shall be destroyed: and who knoweth whether thou art come to the kingdom for such a time as this" (Esther 4:13-14)? Every Great Woman needs to understand she is being prepared by God for a Great Assignment called, "for such a time as this." Like Esther and the Great Women who came before her, and the women God is raising up today, Great Women refuse to allow tradition to box and hem them in; they refuse to allow fear to stop them from being God's ambassadors of change and transformation..

IF I PERISH—I PERISH!

"Then Esther bade them return Mordecai this answer, Go, gather together all the Jews that are present in Shushan, and fast ye for me, and neither eat nor drink three days, night or day: I also and my maidens will fast likewise; and so will I go in unto the king, which is not according to the law: and if I perish, I perish" (Esther 4:15-16). Great Women are not vacillators, hesitaters, and they are certainly not procrastinators. Great Women are women who know how to take decisive action. Once Esther understood the gravity of the threat and the purpose of her strategic positioning, she took immediate action with a radical plan which began with fasting. Fasting indicates that you are serious about afflicting your flesh so God's power can flow through you. Great Women make the sacrifices necessary to fulfill the purpose and plan of God for their lives, and the lives of the people He will use them to impact and/or deliver.

THE THIRD DAY

"Now it came to pass on the third day, that Esther put on her royal apparel, and stood in the inner court of the king's house, over against the king's house: and the king sat upon his royal throne in the royal house, over against the gate of the house. And it was so, when the king saw Esther the queen standing in the court, that she obtained favour in his sight: and the king held out to Esther the golden sceptre that was in his hand. So Esther drew near, and touched the top of the sceptre" (Esther 5:1). The Third Day is a principle in the Bible that represents a day of perfection and completion.

It represents a day when our Lord Jesus Christ will give us complete victory over the enemy. It is also a day when we will stand before our King to hear the words—Well done my good and faithful servant. Esther broke with tradition and made a radical move that saved a nation. Among Jews, women were expected to be quiet, to serve in the home, and to stay on the fringe of religious and political life. But Esther was a Great Woman who broke through the cultural norms, stepping outside her expected role to risk her life to help God's people.

DIG TWO

There is a saying I used to hear when I was growing up-when you are digging a grave, dig two. It means when you are planning the demise of another, you are actually planning your own demise. When Esther exposed Haman's plan to the king, he had him hung on the gallows that had been prepared for Mordecai. Racism will never prevail; evil will never overcome good.

Where are the Esthers of today who refuse to be held down and to give up in defeat? Where are the Great Women who risk their lives by defying the threat of imminent death in defense of preserving the kingdom? Show me the valiant, daring women who will look straight into the eye of their oppressor and subdue and overturn the devices and plans of the enemy. Show me the tenacious, indomitable women who steadfastly refuse to be seated, to be constrained, to be suppressed or silenced concerning moral, ungodly injustice, and are determined to fulfill the plan of God that they were brought to the kingdom to fulfill. They will not allow chauvinistic, misogynistic, religious leaders to abort their vision. Women who will not allow their greatness to be stymied or stifled. There is a company of Great Women like Queen Esther coming forth; their mantra is: "I'm going to see the King. If I perish, I perish!"

DISTINCT QUALITIES OF GREATNESS

- Willing to Risk Everything to See the King
- Refuse to Compromise Integrity
- Not Afraid to Take Risks in Order to Help Others
- Willing to Yield to Preparation for Divine Assignment
- Not Bound by Legalism and Tradition
- Not Afraid to Confront Evil
- Understands the Power and Effectiveness of Prayer and Fasting
- Able to Give Others Coherent Instructions in the Midst of a Crisis
- Humble Enough to Receive Instructions From an Elder

Section Three

POWER, PASSION & PURPOSE IN PRAYER

Hannah

She Needs a Mentor, Not a Tormentor

HANNAH—GAVE BIRTH TO SHIFT A NATION

No one can make you feel inferior without your consent. — Eleanor Roosevelt

The Great woman featured in this chapter is a shining example to all of us of the importance of perseverance and prayer. Her life exemplifies resilience, tenacity and fortitude in the midst of great persecution. She is greatness personified because of her ability to remain meek and humble when she was constantly provoked and misunderstood. Her name is Hannah, which means favor or grace. She was suitably named because she would need both favor and grace to overcome the relentless attack from an adversary living in the same house with her. Jesus stated, "And a man's foes shall be they of his own household" (Matthew 10:36).

Hannah was one of the two wives of a Levite named Elkanah. The other wife Peninnah bore him children, but Hannah was barren. Our present day culture is quite accepting and often times sympathetic towards women who are unable to conceive, but in the then culture one was stigmatized and frowned upon. It was difficult enough to deal with the stigma of barrenness, but in addition to that, Hannah had to deal with persecution and mockery from Peninnah. It is noteworthy that it was socially and culturally acceptable for a man to have more than one wife at that time, but it was not the original plan of God. Remember, the first man Adam was instructed by God to leave his father and mother and cleave to his wife—not wives or concubines. Hannah had to deal with this other wife in the house whose womb was very fertile, while her womb was shut. Instead of showing compassion, Peninnah became her tormentor. Peninnah would be described by self-help guru, Patricia Evans, as a verbally abusive woman. In her highly acclaimed book, *The Verbally Abusive Relationship,* Evans states: "I believe that verbally abusive women have not sought help because they are much more damaged than the average verbally abusive male. They have lost to some degree all that is ascribed to the feminine: their warmth, receptivity, and nurturing qualities, as well as their emotional intelligence. And they have also lost their masculine side: the confidence, self-esteem and action-orientation encouraged in males" (11).

Peninnah's abuse of Hannah came from a place of deep hurt and psychological damage. You may have heard the phrase "hurt people, hurt people." There is no indication that she physically "laid hands" on Hannah; nevertheless, Peninnah abused and tormented poor Hannah until she could take it no longer. You would perhaps expect a woman of that time, and in that polygamous culture, to have sympathy or even empathy, for her sister-wife who had no control over her inability to conceive a child. But jealousy was eating away at Peninnah and instead of comforting Hannah, she lashed out at her and made her misery even more unbearable. The way Hannah handled the toxic environment in which she lived, is a reflection of the greatness on the inside of her and a shining example to all of us.

During that season, the tabernacle which contained the presence of the Lord was at Shiloh, so the family went up to Shiloh every year to worship and to sacrifice unto the Lord. According to the Bible, Elkanah gave portions to Peninnah, her sons and her daughters, but he gave a worthy portion to Hannah because he loved Hannah. In the very next sentence it says—"But the Lord shut up her womb" (1 Samuel 1:4-5). It is important to know when it is the Lord who has shut your womb. When I use the term womb, I am not only referring to the area in the female anatomy where the embryo and the fetus dwell. I am referring to a place or thing that is supposed to facilitate fruitfulness in your life. If you are not able to discern when it is the Lord's doing, you run the risk of thinking it is the devil who is closing your pathways. He will attempt to play tricks on your mind and your emotions to convince you that God has forgotten and forsaken you. Great Women are discerning women who not only perceive God's greater purpose in their situation, but they refuse to succumb to the tormenting spirits sent by the adversary through a Peninnah.

Elkanah was the second son of Korah, a Levite of the line of Heman, the singer. He was a man of wealth and high position, but he could not give Hannah her heart's desire—a son. The love that the Lord has for you is unquestionable, but you must understand there are times and seasons that He will shut things down, so you won't birth out of season. Like Paul and Silas, can you maintain a posture of prayer and praise while you are in prison waiting for your season of fruitfulness to arrive? It doesn't have to be a literal prison. It could be a sickness that imprisons your physical body, or it could be a prison of deep hurt and pain from the betrayal of a spouse who was unfaithful.

It could be a prison of depression and despair from a divorce which left you feeling rejected and abandoned. It could be a mental prison of clinical depression that robs you of your joy and your peace; it could be a financial prison that locks up your finances. While you are waiting on the Lord to take you from barren to bountiful, be of good courage and He will strengthen your heart.

THE SPIRIT OF PENINNAH

"And her adversary also provoked her sore, for to make her fret, because the Lord had shut up her womb" (1 Samuel 1:6). There are times when our English vernacular does not convey the full meaning of what is written in the Bible. In those instances, we must look to the original language to understand what the author intended. In 1 Peter 5:8 the devil is described as an adversary who walks about like a roaring lion seeking whomever he can devour. Peninnah is described as Hannah's adversary, which leads me to believe she was quite a force of evil to be reckoned with. The Hebrew word used for adversary in 1 Samuel 1:6 is the word tsarah, which means tightness, a female rival, affliction, anguish, distress, tribulation, trouble. In Christian circles, you hear a great deal of talk about the spirit of Jezebel, but not about the spirit of Peninnah. The spirit of Peninnah is a relentless persecuting spirit that comes to distress, provoke, and trouble you in the times and seasons when you are in a tight place.

The spirit of Peninnah wages psychological warfare against you in your season of barrenness to weaken and debilitate you. Peninnah did not only provoke Hannah, she tormented her sorely to make her fret. The Hebrew word for fret is ra'am; pronounced (raw-am) and it means to tumble, to be violently agitated, to crash, to irritate with anger. A spirit of torment and persecution was used by the adversary in an attempt to destroy Hannah; But God! "And as he did so year by year, when she went up to the house of the Lord, so she provoked her; therefore, she wept, and did not eat. Then said Elkanah her husband to her, Hannah, why weepest thou? And why eatest thou not? And why is thy heart grieved? Am not I better to thee than ten sons" (1 Samuel 1:7).

Hannah is persecuted in her home and persecuted in the sanctuary to the point where she could not eat. Patricia Evans states: "Verbal abuse is a kind of battering which doesn't leave evidence comparable to the bruises of physical battering. It can be just as painful, and recovery can take much longer" (Evans 15).

Lo-debar represents both a physical and a mental state. "Lo-debar means no pasture; it is a dry place." Rise up and realize **It's Time to Come Out of Lo-debar.** Get in the realm of the Spirit through worship. Worship Him in the midst of your Midnight. Worship Him in the intense heat and pressure, knowing you are *a diamond in the rough.*

Hannah refused to be petty and vengeful. She had her moments of sorrow, but like all Great Women, she kept the focus on God. Great Women are not lured into lurid and carnal conversations with the concubines who have seduced their husbands, because they know the weapons of their warfare are not carnal and they wrestle not against flesh and blood. They refuse to stay in a place or a state of despair. Hannah rose up and prayed to the Lord. She was in bitterness of soul and wept sorely, but she understood the power of prayer. She lost her appetite for food, but did not lose her appetite for prayer. At times, bitterness of soul can have you in a place where you lose your appetite for food, but do not, I repeat, do not lose your appetite for prayer. Luke 18:1 states, "And he spake a parable unto them to this end, that men ought always to pray, and not to faint." Prayer is your power tool. It is the jack hammer that allows you to break up the fallow ground. You are a Great Woman like Naomi and Hannah, so I exhort you in the name of the Lord Jesus Christ to rise up, fast and pray until you receive your deliverance.

MISUNDERSTOOD BY LEADERSHIP—EVER BEEN THERE?

Things didn't get easier for Hannah when she decided to pray. When the enemy sees that you have chosen prayer over pity and worship over worry, he will intensify the attack. "Now Eli the priest sat upon a seat by a post of the temple of the Lord. And she was in bitterness of soul, and prayed unto the Lord, and wept sore. And she vowed a vow, and said, O Lord of hosts, if thou wilt indeed look on the affliction of thine handmaid, and remember me, and not forget thine handmaid, but wilt give unto thine handmaid a man child, then I will give him unto the Lord all the days of his life, and there shall no razor come upon his head" (1 Samuel 1:10-11). Hannah didn't pray for a man child so she could keep him for herself. She prayed for a man child so that she could dedicate Him to the Lord. "And it came to pass, as she continued praying before the Lord, that Eli marked her mouth. Now Hannah, she spake in her heart; only her lips moved, but her voice was not heard" (1 Samuel 1:12-13).

She was praying from a place of such deep sorrow that her mouth moved, but no sound came out. Have you ever been there? When Jesus was in anguish in the Garden of Gethsemane while in prayer, His sweat was like drops of blood. Therefore, Eli thought she was drunk. Tormented and persecuted in her home and in the sanctuary by Peninnah, now she was misunderstood by leadership. Great women can deal with multiple attacks and maintain a posture of prayer. "And Eli said unto her, how long wilt thou be drunken? Put away thy wine from thee." By now you would think she would have blown a fuse and given a fleshy outburst, but listen to her response. She remained poised in the midst of pressure. Patience in the midst of persecution; that is what Great Women exude. They are not catty, they pray with maturity. "And Hannah answered and said, No, my lord, I am a woman of a sorrowful spirit: I have drunk neither wine nor strong drink, but have poured out my soul before the Lord" (1 Samuel 1:15). Can you fight the urge to give a fleshly response to your accusers and pour out your soul to the Lord when your spirit is sorrowful? She told Eli, "Count not thine handmaid for a daughter of Belial: for out of the abundance of my complaint and grief have I spoken hitherto" (1 Samuel 1:16). When you feel as if the battle is at its hottest, intensify your prayer to the Lord because He will hear your cry and vindicate you.

Like Sarah and Rachel, Hannah grieved over the children she couldn't have. But unlike them, she took her anguish directly to God. Misunderstood by both her husband and her priest, she could easily have turned her sorrow on herself or others, becoming bitter, hopeless, or vindictive. But instead of merely pitying herself or responding in kind, she poured out her soul to God. And God graciously answered her prayer (Women of the Bible, 147) "Then Eli answered and said, Go in peace: and the God of Israel grant thee thy petition that thou hast asked of him. And she said, Let thine handmaid find grace in thy sight" (1 Samuel 1:17). It is not easy to hold your peace when you are tormented and falsely accused of being drunk, but if you hold your peace and keep the focus on God, He will cause your accusers to speak a blessing over you. Once Eli blessed her she went her way and did eat; and her countenance was no more sad. "And they rose up in the morning early, and worshipped before the Lord, and returned, and came to their house to Ramah" (1 Samuel 1:19). As was previously stated, Ramah means, an elevated place. Hannah went from a place of barrenness and deep sorrow to a place of elevation and fruitfulness because she understood **the power of persistent prayer.** It is the type of prayer that produces results, and causes a change in your countenance.

"And Elkanah knew Hannah his wife; and the Lord remembered her. Wherefore it came to pass, when the time was come about after Hannah had conceived, that she bare a son, and called his name Samuel, saying, Because I have asked him of the Lord" (1 Samuel 1:20).

PRAYER + INTIMATE WORSHIP=CONCEPTION

Hannah went into the temple to pray and worship, then went home for a time of intimacy with her husband. That combination produced fruit in her womb. Contrast Hannah with David's wife, Michal, who excoriated the King and accused him of disrobing himself before the maidens when he was in a deep place of worship before the Lord. Her actions caused her womb to be barren. After giving birth, Hannah weaned her son, Samuel. She kept her word by dedicating him to the house of the Lord after the weaning period. Can you imagine the courage it took to release him to the service of the Lord after she had endured years of infertility, persecution, deep sorrow and cried so many tears? Her actions were further evidence of the Greatness on the inside of her. When you get to the place where you can release that thing to the Lord that is most precious, like Abraham who was willing to release Isaac, like Hannah did with Samuel, like our Father in Heaven who gave us His only begotten Son, Jesus Christ, we will hear the words Abraham heard from the Lord. "Now I know that thou fearest God, seeing thou hast not withheld thy son, thine only son from me" (Genesis 22:12). Then we will know the LORD as Jehovah Jireh; the Lord God our Provider. I love the way 1 Samuel 2:1 starts, "And Hannah prayed." She prayed in the midst of persecution and sorrow and did not forget God when she received her breakthrough. She continued to pray. Prayer must permeate and saturate our lives. Hannah said, "My heart rejoiceth in the Lord, mine horn is exalted in the Lord: my mouth is enlarged over mine enemies; because I rejoice in thy salvation. There is none holy as the Lord: for there is none beside thee: neither is there any rock like our God" (1 Samuel 2:1-2). That Rock is Jesus and He is Solid. She couldn't articulate her previous prayers in words because of the depth of sorrow in her spirit, but this time it is a prayer of celebration for her victory.

WHERE ARE THE HANNAHS?

I was speaking with my good friend and brother in the Lord, Attorney Michael Valentine, and he dropped a few priceless nuggets on me. He said, "Out of her, pain and sorrow, Hannah birthed the one who would transition the nation from the old to the new; from the status quo to the divine flow; from disorder to divine order." The last verse of the book of Judges reads, "In those days there was no king in Israel: every man did that which was right in his own eyes" (Judges 21:25). The nation went from being a theocracy to anarchy. They needed a divine paradigm shift and God held Hannah's womb in protective custody until it was time to conceive and birth Samuel—the anointer of kings who walked in a three-fold anointing of prophet, priest and judge. Conception comes through intimacy—birthing comes through contractions. Conception requires an act—birthing requires process.

Under Eli's leadership the people turned away from the temple because they were being extorted by his sons Hophni and Phineas. The priests profited through extortion: rich pastors and impoverished congregations. They were Levitical priests who were enriching themselves with the proceeds from the church offering. Because of their actions, the Bible declares, men abhorred the offering of the LORD. Their debauchery did not stop at the stealing of church money; they had sex with women who assembled at the door of the church. God sent a man of God to tell Eli that both his sons would die on the same day, and He would raise up a faithful priest that would do according to that which was in His heart and mind. Hannah's womb would be privileged to birth that son, but she had to endure the persecution and the misunderstanding. Her desperation for a son was birthed out of her desperation to see her nation transformed. That is why she planned to dedicate him to the LORD. Again, I ask the question: where are the Hannahs who are willing to endure suffering, willing to turn down their plates and pray, so God can birth a nation-transformer out of them? Are you praying self-centered prayers, or are you praying nation-transforming prayers? Great Women like Hannah pray, conceive and birth out destiny changers and destiny shapers.

Distinct Qualities of Greatness

- Meek and Humble
- Brokenness in the Presence of the Lord
- Inner Strength
- Depth in Prayer
- Gives Her Best to the Lord
- Remains Focused When Persecuted and Misunderstood
- Epitomizes Perseverance
- Promise Keeper
- Receives Elder's Rebuke without Succumbing to the Flesh

Chapter 8

Anna

Age is Just a Number

ANNA—KINGDOM DEDICATION

strong woman works out every day to keep her body in shape, but a woman of strength kneels in prayer to keep her soul in shape.—www.iamblessed.com

Ever so often I hear someone say, "you are as young as you feel." The Bible declares, "Through faith also Sara herself received strength to conceive seed, and was delivered of a child when she was past age, because she judged him faithful who had promised" (Hebrews 11:11). Age should not be used as an excuse for a lack of kingdom productivity. Sarah was able to conceive and deliver an Isaac because she judged God faithful who promised to make her barren womb fruitful.

AGE IS JUST A NUMBER

The Great Woman, Anna, was used mightily by God at an age when some would think she should have been in a senior citizen's center. Her story is one of steadfast dedication to the temple, prayer and fasting. God will do exploits in the life of any person who has a zeal for His house, for prayer and for fasting, irrespective of age or any other thing that is deemed a liability. Before we examine the life and ministry of the Great Woman, Anna, please allow me to give you some Biblical information on some things that took place prior to her encounter with Jesus in the temple; an encounter which took place when He was a new born babe. "And when eight days were accomplished for the circumcising of the child, his name was called JESUS, which was so named of the angel before he was conceived in the womb. And when the days of her purification according to the law of Moses were accomplished, they brought him to Jerusalem, to present him to the Lord; (As it is written in the law of the Lord, every male that openeth the womb shall be called holy to the Lord" (Luke 2:21-30).

TELL THEM THE COMFORTER HAS COME

I would imagine there were many parents bringing their new born sons to the temple to be dedicated at the time when Baby Jesus was brought there. I would also imagine that some of them had the name Yeshua like He did. The difference between Jesus and the others was;

He was born Son of God, He was born King, and He was born Savior and Redeemer. When Mary and Joseph brought Him into the temple, they encountered a just and devout man named Simeon. The Holy Ghost was upon him and he waited for the consolation of Israel. One of the Greek definitions of the word consolation is comforter. Jesus would eventually tell His disciples that when He departed, He would pray to the Father and He would send them another Comforter.

The name Simeon means hearing; he had a keen spiritual ear and discernment. Simeon was elderly at that time and he had waited all his life, prayed and had faith that he would not leave the earth before he saw the Messiah. The Holy Ghost honored his request and revealed to him that he would not see death, before he had seen the Lord's Christ. When the Holy Ghost is on you, revelation will come to you. Jesus told Peter, "Blessed art thou, Simon Barjona: for flesh and blood hath not revealed it unto thee, but my Father which is in heaven" (Matthew 16:17). What was revealed to Peter? It was revealed to him that Jesus is the Christ. Simeon came by the leading of the Spirit into the temple at the precise time Mary and Joseph brought Jesus. When Simeon saw them, he took Jesus in his arms; he blessed Him and asked the Lord to let him depart in peace in fulfillment of the word God had spoken to him, because his eyes had seen God's salvation. Whenever you have an encounter with Jesus, you will depart that place with peace because He is the Prince of Peace.

AN ENCOUNTER OF THE DIVINE KIND

After the encounter with Simeon, Joseph, Mary and Baby Jesus had a second profound encounter, this one with the Great Woman, Anna. Like the Great Woman, Hannah, her name also means grace and she had a dedicated prayer life. Anna is one of the women in the Bible that is recognized as a prophetess. She is described in the Bible as being of a great age, and had lived with her husband seven years from her virginity. This means, she married as a young virgin and lived with her husband for seven years before he died leaving her a widow. She was widowed for eighty-four years, so if you add those years to the seven years she was married, Anna was over one hundred years old.

GET YOUR FLESH IN CHECK

After the death of her husband, Anna didn't go out looking for a Boaz. She was still young, but she kept her flesh in check and the Bible tells us something about her (in Luke 2:37) that reinforces my argument that Anna was a Great Woman. She departed not from the temple, but served God with fastings and prayers, night and day. When tragedy strikes, some folks quit the church, they backslide, they start acting and talking crazy, they blame God, they get in the flesh and start doing all kinds of carnal things. After seven years of marriage and her husband dies leaving her a young widow, Anna does not blame God and turn her back on Him. On the contrary, she goes deeper into His presence by her dedication. She was constantly in the temple ministering to the Lord and to His people. Through that level of consecration and dedication to fasting and prayer, she flowed in a heavy prophetic oil, and like Simeon, she was very sensitive to the Holy Ghost. Distractions will come and tragic situations will hit your life, but the question that must be asked of you is, will you allow the loss of a loved one or some other tragedy to hinder and distract you from the great calling that is on your life?

I'm sure Anna took the time to mourn, but instead of retreating to a dark place of depression, she made a choice to dedicate herself to God as a consecrated vessel to be used for His glory. I remember when my grandson died before he came out of the hospital and I had to encourage my daughter. I reminded her of the time when King David had a child who was sick to the point of death. David fasted, prayed and prostrated himself upon the earth all night as he sought the LORD. When the child died, His servants were afraid to inform him. When he found out the child was dead, he arose from the earth, washed and anointed himself, changed his apparel, and came into the house of the LORD, and worshipped. Then he went to his own house and ate.

Some people would go home first, go in their room, close the blinds, stop taking calls, pull the cover over their heads and sink into deep depression. David rose up, Ezekiel rose up after the death of his wife, Naomi rose up after the death of her husband and sons, Anna rose up after the death of her husband, and you can too.

While writing this chapter, I had the opportunity to minister at a local church and there was a great move of God in the service. I woke up the next morning to be met with news via a text that my wife received, that our son was stabbed in his stomach and was rushed into emergency surgery because he almost bled to death. During the service, I made reference to the Prophet Ezekiel and his dedication and obedience to what God had called him to do in the midst of a tragedy.

"Also the word of the Lord came unto me, saying, Son of man, behold, I take away from thee the desire of thine eyes with a stroke: yet neither shalt thou mourn nor weep, neither shall thy tears run down. Forbear to cry, make no mourning for the dead, bind the tire of thine head upon thee, and put on thy shoes upon thy feet, and cover not thy lips, and eat not the bread of men. So I spake unto the people in the morning: and at even my wife died; and I did in the morning as I was commanded" (Ezekiel 24:15-18). The Prophet is informing the reader that he did what the Lord commanded and His wife died. Obedience to the will of God will not exempt or give us a free pass from tragedy. While executing our respective ministries, people are going to die, they will divorce us and they will forsake us. Job was a perfect man who feared God and eschewed evil, yet he lost all his children tragically. But Job was able to arise from the ash heap. So, also, must you be steadfast and resolute like the Great Women and Great Men who are shining examples of obedience to the will of our Heavenly Father.

THE FAST THE LORD HAS CHOSEN

Anna fasted night and day and that must have been challenging. However, when you are dedicated to God, He will give you the grace to endure, and the strength to accomplish what He needs you to do. It wasn't the kind of fast many people do today like the one they call the Daniel Fast—where they abstain from certain types of food like sweets, eat vegetables and drink water or drink fruit juice. Unfortunately, that is a diet not a fast. Daniel and the others were placed on a special diet. The Hebrew word for Fast means to shut or cover the mouth. When Queen Esther sent word for all the Jews to fast, and she and her maidens would fast also, she mentioned that she would neither eat nor drink for three days. That is the crux of what fasting is all about.

She did the kind of fasting that Ezra references in the book that bears his name. Ezra 8:21: "Then I proclaimed a fast there, at the river of Ahava, that we might afflict ourselves before our God, to seek of him a right way for us, and for our little ones, and for all our substance." The kind of fast that Nehemiah did when Hanani told him about the condition of the Jews that had escaped, which were left of the captivity, and concerning Jerusalem.

Nehemiah 1:3-4 states, "And they said unto me, The remnant that are left of the captivity there in the province are in great affliction and reproach:

the wall of Jerusalem also is broken down, and the gates thereof are burned with fire. And it came to pass, when I heard these words, that I sat down and wept, and mourned certain days, and fasted, and prayed before the God of heaven." The type of fast Jesus spoke about in Matthew 17:21 when He declared, "Howbeit this kind goeth not out but by prayer and fasting." When the wall has a breach the enemy will penetrate. Fasting and prayer keeps the walls of our lives fortified. Fasting and prayer will break the grip of strong demonic spirits.

I KNOW MY REDEEMER LIVES

That is the kind of fasting and prayer the Great Woman, Anna did. She didn't serve God with lip service and no action. She wasn't serving Him for what she could get out of it. She didn't cut and run when things got tough after she became a young widow. She served God with fasting and prayers, night and day, which caused her to live in a great spiritual dimension. You cannot afflict your flesh in that manner and not operate in great spiritual power. In other words, sacrificing your body by denying it food, gives your spirit a chance to focus on spiritual matters, instead of on matters of the flesh. It also allows the Holy Spirit to complete His work within you. God acknowledged Anna's faithfulness and bestowed special honor upon her on one of the occasions that she visited the temple. Like Simeon, she was able to see Jesus at His dedication and give thanks to God. She spoke of Him to everyone in Jerusalem who looked for redemption. The divine encounter was personal for Simeon—he wanted to see the Messiah before he died, but Anna made a public, prophetic proclamation, announcing that the Redeemer had arrived. Like Simeon, she was able to see, through discernment from the Holy Spirit, that the child brought to the temple to be dedicated by His parents was not just any child, but the gift given by God for the redemption of many. Simeon saw Yeshua as Comforter, Anna saw Him as Redeemer—how do you see Him?

Like Anna, dedicate yourself to Almighty God through deep dedication and consecration, and you will flow in a potent, prophetic oil and Holy Ghost discernment. Great Women are overcomers with a high level of commitment to the presence of Almighty God. His anointing oil flows out of them through prayer and prophesy because they are willing to afflict their souls through a constant posture of fasting. They operate in a high level of piety and purity which allows them to have the prophetic eyes of Eagles.

FOR THERE SHALL BE A PERFORMANCE!

"And when they had performed all things according to the law of the Lord, they returned into Galilee, to their own city Nazareth. And the child grew, and waxed strong in spirit, filled with wisdom: and the grace of God was upon him" (Luke 2:39-40). If you desire to grow and wax strong in spirit like Jesus; if you want to be filled with wisdom and have the grace of God upon you like Jesus, then dedicate yourself more to His Presence. Fast and pray constantly, get and stay connected to people who are flowing in consecration and prophetic Holy Ghost oil like Anna.

DISTINCT QUALITIES OF GREATNESS

- Steadfast Dedication to the Temple of God
- Deep Commitment to Fasting and Prayer
- Prophetic Voice to Her Nation
- Self -Denial
- A Servant of God
- Thanksgiving
- Age: Not an Issue
- Gender: Not an Issue
- Deep Love for God

Lydia

Pray or You Will Be the Devil's Prey

LYDIA—TRANSFORMATIONAL PRAYER

very great dream begins with a dreamer—always remember, you have within you the strength, the patience, and the passion to reach for the stars, to change the world. —Harriet Tubman

My book Midnight is based on the prayer and praise sent up to God by Paul and Silas when they were in the inner prison in Philippi. Their feet were fastened with stocks and they were probably beaten before they were thrown into prison. Paul and Silas arrived in Philippi through the leading of the Holy Spirit because of what is commonly known as a Macedonian Call. The Macedonian Call is an assignment that one receives from the Lord through prayer. "And a vision appeared to Paul in the night; There stood a man of Macedonia, and prayed him, saying, Come over into Macedonia, and help us. And after he had seen the vision, immediately we endeavored to go into Macedonia, assuredly gathering that the Lord had called us for to preach the gospel unto them" (Acts 16:9-10). They arrived in Philippi, the chief city of that part of Macedonia, the colony, and abided many days there. The protocol when Paul and his companions traveled in a new city was to find a synagogue and preach Christ to the Jews as the gospel was to go to the Jews first. There was no synagogue in the city, but there were arches outside of the city with an inscription prohibiting anyone from bringing in any unrecognized religion. Paul knew he was in the city by divine directive, so he tarried and waited on the Holy Ghost. It is very difficult to fulfill God's assignment without patience. When He gives you an assignment, be patient, and follow the leading of the Holy Spirit.

GREAT WOMEN ARE PRAYING WOMEN

On the Sabbath they went out of the city to a riverside. When you are on an assignment for God, you have to be ready to go outside of the norm, outside of what is comfortable. What they found when they went outside the city would facilitate the transformation of not only Philippi, and Macedonia, but the continent of Europe. Down by the riverside they encountered a group of women praying. The prayer meeting was led by a Great Woman named Lydia. Persistence pays dividends, and that is why Great Women are relentless when it comes to prayer.

There was no synagogue in the city, the Gospel had not been preached there so there was no church established, but Great Women were praying. When Great Women come together to pray, transformation is going to take place. Transformation takes place because they don't allow anything negative to break their ranks; Paul and his companions sat down and spoke to the women who did not know when they gathered for prayer that day, that their lives would be changed forever. You never know when the increase is going to come, but you should know beyond a shadow of a doubt, that if you remain faithful, it shall manifest.

A SUCCESSFUL BUSINESS WOMAN

Lydia came to Philippi from Thyatira and was a seller of purple (purple dyes for fabrics). The inhabitants of Thyatira were celebrated for their proficiency in dyeing. Purple cloth was valuable and expensive, and often worn as a sign of nobility. Lydia was financially independent because of her successful import business. She was able to afford an establishment at Philippi that was large enough to accommodate the missionary party. She was not a Jewess, but a proselyte (Proselyte: A convert to Judaism).

WORSHIPPER OF GOD

Lydia was a worshipper of God who had a persistent prayer life and when you adopt that kind of posture, heaven will respond. Heaven responded when the Holy Ghost led Paul and his team to the city and the Lord honored Lydia by opening her heart to receive His word from Paul's mouth. With an attentive ear and an open heart, she attended unto the things which were spoken by Paul. Prayer should not be a monologue or a one-way conversation. People who are dedicated to prayer know they have to be good listeners so they can hear God's answer. Lydia didn't have a revelation of Messiah, but her consistent prayer life coupled with her worship, brought the revelation of Him to her prayer meeting. When you are a worshipper, your ears will be opened and calibrated to the sound of the Gospel, and your heart will be opened to receive it.

Among her other great attributes, Lydia was a pioneer, a trailblazer and a trendsetter because she was the first person in Europe who embraced Christianity. What an awesome distinction to hold: being the first person on a continent to hear and embrace the Gospel of the Kingdom.

Once she received Christ she was baptized with her household. Your faithfulness does not only facilitate Kingdom impact on your life, but on your household and the people who are connected to you. She asked Paul if he judged her to be faithful, to come into her house and abide there (Luke said she constrained him). This is not the first time a man of God was constrained by a Great Woman; remember, the prophet Elisha was constrained by the Great Woman of Shunem to enter her house to eat bread. The fellowship eventually led to an addition being built on her house large enough to give rest to the prophet and his servant. The Greek word for constrained is, parabiazomai (pronounced par-ab-ee-ad-zom-ahee); it means to force, to compel. I'm sure Lydia, like the Great Woman of Shunem, was a woman of great respect and dignity, but when it came to blessing the men of God, they were very determined.

Prayer is a common theme evidenced in the lives of men and women in the Bible, and in the Body of Christ. So, it is not surprising that Paul and his team continued to keep their focus on prayer after being used by the Holy Ghost to plant the church in Philippi. After all, it was prayer in the form of the Macedonian Call that the Holy Ghost used to lead them to the city and It was the prayer meeting they attended by the riverside that connected them to Lydia and the other women. Acts 16:16 states: "And it came to pass, as we went to prayer, a certain damsel possessed with a spirit of divination met us, which brought her masters much gain by soothsaying." The spirit of divination operating in and through the damsel became an irritant to Paul and his team, because she followed them crying out, "these men are the servants of the most high God, which show unto us the way of salvation." She did that for many days, which must have been distracting, and very irritating. What she said was true and sounded good, but it is not God's will for the Gospel to be spread through a spirit of divination. Fortune-tellers know there is a God, they just decide not to renounce their craft, and yield to Him. The damsel was a distraction to Paul, so he cast the spirit out of her.

The damsel's masters were not pleased and had Paul and Silas thrown into prison. Instead of lamenting what had befallen them, they turned their cell into a place of prayer and praise unto God. The prayer and praise transformed the atmosphere in the prison and caused a great earthquake to shake the prison's foundations. When the foundation was shaken, every prisoner's door was opened and the jailer attempted to draw his sword to kill himself, but Paul stopped him. As a result the jailer and his household were saved that day.

It is amazing what was accomplished by God through Paul and his team in Philippi through the Macedonian Prayer Call, and the encounter with the Great Woman, Lydia, and her prayer meeting. When they left the prison they went back to Lydia's house and rested, then left the area for their next assignment. I encourage Great Women all over the world who have committed themselves to prayer, to know that your labor in prayer is not in vain. Stay consistent and persistent in prayer like Lydia, for in due season you will witness the fruits of your labor.

DISTINCT QUALITIES OF GREATNESS

- Entrepreneur
- Kingdom Funder
- Committed to Prayer
- Pliable Heart
- Wealthy but Humble Enough to Serve
- Opened Her Home to the Servants of the Lord
- Allowed Herself to be Used by God to Transform a Continent
- Humility
- Faithful

Section Four

THE PROPHETIC ENCOUNTER

The Widow of Zarephath

Last, but Not Least

THE WIDOW OF ZAREPHATH—LAST SHALL BE FIRST

Here's to strong women. May we know them. May we be them. May we raise them. —Source Unknown.

Widows occupy a special place in the heart and plan of God; His concern for them is clearly stated in the Bible. Psalm 68:5 declares, "A father of the fatherless, and a judge of the widows, is God in his holy habitation." The book of James confirms this. Pure religion and undefiled before God and the Father is this, "To visit the fatherless and widows in their affliction, and to keep himself unspotted from the world" (James 1:27).

WHEN STRANGERS MEET—THE POWER OF FELLOWSHIP

God's Great Women come from all walks of life and varying faith levels. 1 Kings 17 records the story of Elijah the prophet being sent by God to hide himself by the brook, Cherith. His meals were supplied by ravens, and his water source was the brook. When the brook dried up because of a lack of rain, God instructed him to arise and go to a to a city called Zarephath, to dwell there. A widow woman was commanded by God to sustain him at a time when she faced an existential crisis. It was a command that would challenge and transform her life. Her response to the challenge qualifies her as one of the Great Women in my hall of faith.

I was not only intrigued by the places God sent the prophet, but also by the sources used to sustain him. Ravens are considered dirty birds who don't care for their young, and widows need help in good times, so their conditions would be more egregious in a time of drought and famine. There are times when God's instructions will not make sense in the natural; in those times, you must walk by faith and not by sight. Great Women are women of faith; they have the strength and fortitude to face life's threatening challenges, and still fulfill the will of God.

Zarephath was located in the territory ruled by Jezebel's father, a territory dominated by Baal worship. Although she lived in an area dominated by Baal worship, the widow's life was lived in a manner that God saw fit to use her to sustain His prophet. What is notable about the widow is, despite her desperate situation, she received a stranger, someone not like herself.

Moreover, she put herself at risk by harboring the prophet that God used to speak to King Ahab concerning the withholding of rain. The lack of rainfall was the judgment of God upon His people for forsaking Him in favor of Baal. The widow was a jewel, a gem in a spiritually dark society. She exemplified generosity, hospitality, and bravery, all of which are qualities possessed by Great Women. When Elijah arrived at the gate of the city, the widow was there gathering sticks to start a fire in-order to prepare her last meal. God is a God of precise timing. His word will not return unto Him void; it must accomplish the divine purpose He sends it to accomplish, and it must prosper in those things.

When asked by Elijah for a drink of water she acquiesced, but when asked to provide a morsel of bread, she responded: "As surely as the LORD your God lives, I don't have any bread—only a handful of flour in a jar and a little olive oil in a jug. I am gathering a few sticks to take home and make a meal for myself and my son, that we may eat it–and die" (1 Kings 17:12). She was living in the land of Baal worship, but she knew that the God of Elijah was the living God. That knowledge gave her the courage and conviction to obey God's divine directive through His prophet. Elijah told her not to fear, but to do exactly as she said, only make his first. Afterwards he told her of the blessing from the Lord that would follow her obedience. Great Women are able to overcome the spirit of fear, and manifest acts of kindness in the midst of extraordinary circumstances.

Understand the posture of the widow. Protection of widows was the universal, social policy throughout the Near East. However, it seems that societal norm was cast aside during times of national crisis and this would have made her quite vulnerable. Due to the famine in the land, which was as a result of the drought, we find this widow with only a handful of flour and a little olive oil. She had no known protector and could not rely on her young son for support. Yet, under the circumstances, she was doing the best she could with the little she possessed. In her hopelessness and vulnerable state, she was not looking for a personal prophecy or any other word from God. In her transparency, she acknowledged that she knew the name of the LORD, but that she did not serve the living God. In spite of that lack of knowledge, she trusted the integrity of the word of instruction from God's prophet.

When Elijah told her to make his bread first, he was not being selfish. He understood the Kingdom principle that Jesus would later reveal according to Matthew 6:33.

When God is first, things will come into alignment. The widow only had enough for herself and her son, and Elijah instructed her to make his first. The instructions did not appear to be in her favor from a basic mathematical principle and it certainly wasn't logical. However, God's power is not limited by man's mathematics or logic; His growth is exponential. The widow's obedience activated the power principle of the number three. According to Ecclesiastes 4:12; a threefold cord is not easily broken. 1 Corinthians 3:6 states, "I have planted, Apollos watered; but God gave the increase." It was a sacrifice for the widow, but obedience is better than sacrifice. In the natural, she only had enough for two, but obedience to the prophetic word caused a shift from natural to supernatural. When the prophetic word was injected into the equation, what was only sufficient for two, multiplied as the heavens opened over the widow's household when she obeyed the words found in 2 Chronicles 20:20. "Believe in the Lord your God, so shall ye be established; believe his prophets, so shall ye prosper."

The widow's obedience to the divine instructions opened the door for the prophetic word concerning multiplication of her meager resources. The essence of the divine instruction for the widow was that she had to enter into fellowship with Elijah without regard for the personal cost. By entering into fellowship with Elijah, the LORD, who is the Creator of heaven and earth, is able to create more out of a little. At the core of fellowship is unconstrained sharing of sustenance. When two strangers meet as ordained by God, and move beyond judgment based on religious mores and societal norms, the creative word of God is manifested.

The Great Expositor, Jesus himself, shared with us a very interesting revelation about the fellowship between Elijah and the widow. Jesus assured His listeners that there were many widows in Israel in Elijah's time, when the heavens were shut for three and a half years and there was a severe famine throughout the land. Yet, Elijah was not sent to any of them, but to a widow in Zarephath. The point Jesus was demonstrating is: no prophet is accepted in his hometown. A prophet is accepted by strangers who do not know God and for that reason the strangers receive a greater blessing.

Like the Shunammite woman, the widow of Zarephath was a woman of discernment. She was able to recognize, and to discern that Elijah was a man of God. Little becomes much when it is released into the hands of a true man or woman of God and that is why you cannot be intimidated when a true prophet asks you to do something that challenges your faith and causes your flesh to scream. When the five fish and two loaves were put into the hands of Jesus, the true Master Prophet, multiplication took place and five thousand men plus women and children were fed, with enough left-over to fill twelve baskets. The widow, in 2 Kings 4, had creditors banging on her door to take away her two sons because of her debt, but an encounter with the Prophet Elisha took her from famine to feast. Make sure you are connected to a true prophet of God, and don't be afraid to release substance into his or her hands, even if it is your last. The widow who encountered Elisha had a pot of oil and the widow of Zarephath had a handful of meal and a little oil. Though both were minimal, they were enough to facilitate a miracle. It is not the size of what you have, but your obedience that makes the difference. You will know when God's purpose is fueling the sacrifice you are making by the size of the blessing you receive. That is not to say you are doing it for a blessing. However, God has already shown you in these biblical narratives that He does not ask us to make sacrifices without multiplying our storehouses above and beyond what we could even ask for.

BE WILLING AND OBEDIENT

Great Women don't allow the magnitude of the prophetic instructions to shrink their faith; on the contrary, they always choose faith over fear. The prophetic word from the mouth of the Lord will come to pass once the recipient is obedient. The severity of your situation will not negate the authenticity of God's word. God's love for you is perfect and that perfect love will cast out all fear. Once fear is cast out, you are free to obey the word and the word always produces fruit in the lives of His children.

THE PROPHET'S REWARD—FROM FAMINE TO FEAST

"He that receiveth a prophet in the name of a prophet shall receive a prophet's reward; and he that receiveth a righteous man in the name of a righteous man shall receive a righteous man's reward" (Matthew 10:41). The widow's obedience brought a torrential rain fall of blessing to her household, but the blessing did not stop there. Her son died while the prophet was there and he was able to raise him from the dead by the power of God.

I was listening in on the Chain Breakers Prayer Line while typing this section of the manuscript for this book. An anointed prophetess named Lakesha Savage was ministering and she released a nugget that blessed me tremendously. She told the listeners, "It will be unprofitable for you if you don't give something to the prophet." Great women, like the widow of Zarephath, understood this revelation; not only was the widow willing to bless Elijah, she was willing to do it with her last. It is easy to give from a place of comfort, but when you give out of your little, out of your last, great things will manifest in your life. We see this principle not only with the widow of Zarephath, but with the widow Jesus saw when she put her two mites into the treasury. There were many rich people who were casting money into the treasury at that time, but Jesus took note of the poor widow as she threw in her two mites, which made a farthing, and used it as a teachable moment for His disciples. He told them, "And he said, Of a truth I say unto you, that this poor widow hath cast in more than they all: For all these have of their abundance cast in unto the offerings of God: but she of her penury hath cast in all the living that she had." (Luke 21:3-4)

Great Women will give up their last to advance the Kingdom of God. That widow did not have an easy life; this assertion is evidenced by the fact that Jesus said she was a poor widow. I truly believe she never lacked after that because Jesus rewards faithfulness. I know increase and overflow came to her house after that radical move in her giving. She came into the temple a poor widow, but her willingness to give up her last caused Jesus to notice her and when Jesus notices your giving, increase will come to your living.

DISTINCT QUALITIES OF GREATNESS

- Great Caretaker
- Ability to Discern
- Poised Under Pressure
- Altruistic
- Radical in her Giving
- Sustained the Man of God
- Willing and Obedient
- Put the Kingdom First
- Humble

The Shunammite Woman

A Gem Cannot be Polished Without Friction-Nor a Great Woman Perfected Without Trials

THE SHUNAMMITE WOMAN—THE CHAZAQ ANOINTING

tudy the lives of our Great Women who are models of patience, fortitude, compassion and sacrifice. —Sathya Sai Baba

I was fascinated with this woman's story from the first time I read it.To be called a Great Woman in the times and culture in which she lived, meant she was indeed exceptional.

When I read the title Great Woman, I knew she had to possess some distinguishing, meritorious qualities. She is not named, but out of one hundred and eighty eight women in the Bible, she is the only one with that illustrious, exclusive, and legendary title. All biblical names have meaning and representation of character. They are self-fulfilling prophecies either positively or negatively; favorably or unfavorably. I often think, the Shunammite woman was not given a name for a specific reason; God does not do anything randomly or perfunctory.

The Shunammite woman was a prosperous, generous, spiritually mature woman who lived in a little village of Issachar named Shunem, which means rest or quiet. She had an encounter with the Prophet Elisha when he passed her village on one of his prophetic missions. Through astute assessment and the ability to recognize that Elisha was not just any ordinary man, she provided accommodations and provision for him. Her story is told in 2 Kings Chapter 4 and Chapter 8. 2 Kings Chapter 4:8 states: "And it fell on a day, that Elisha passed to Shunem, where was a great woman; and she constrained him to eat bread. And so it was, that as oft as he passed by, he turned in thither to eat bread."

As the story of the Shunammite woman unfolds, you will see her character, her fortitude, and her tenacity; you will understand why she was designated as Great in the Bible. It is quite fitting that the prophet would be constrained by a Great Woman in a resting place, providing comfort for him as he executed the work of the Lord. The woman of Shunem is another example of a woman of action who refused to be boxed in or kept in a certain place because of her gender. Like all Great Women, she was a very wise woman equipped with exceptional talents, and bearing the gift of a spirit of discernment and determination. She was not only able to discern, but was willing to act on that discernment and do so, radically.

The word constrained represents a very important Biblical Kingdom Principle, which when it is understood and acted upon, will produce manifold blessings. The Hebrew word for constrained is chazaq, pronounced; (khaw-zak') and it means, to fasten upon; to seize, to be strong, to be courageous and to strengthen; all definitive terms that appropriately apply to the Shunammite woman.

She purposed in her heart to bless the prophet and refused to take no for an answer. This is indicative of her perseverance and signifies a prevailing quality of a very strong and assured woman. Imagine someone being that energized and determined in order to show kindness to another. The hospitality was so good, Elisha stopped at her house to eat whenever he was in the village. At some point she went to her husband and said, "Behold now, I perceive that this is an holy man of God, which passeth by us continually" (2 Kings 4:9). Having him as a regular guest gave her the opportunity to further observe and discern his character. The first and greatest attribute she displayed was her determination to extend hospitality; going over and beyond what is required. The next great attribute we see in her is her perception. The first thing she perceived about Elisha was not that he was a prophet, but that he was a holy man of God. There are some who desire an elevated position; to be conferred with a five-fold title to be placed before their name, but how many desire to be recognized as holy? Hebrews 12:14 does not say, follow peace with all men, and prophecy, without which no man shall see the Lord. It says: "Follow peace with all men, and holiness, without which no man shall see the Lord." 1 Peter 1:15-16 declares: "But as he which hath called you is holy, so be ye holy in all manner of conversation; Because it is written, Be ye holy; for I am holy."

WOMAN'S INTUITION OR SPIRITUAL PERCEPTION?

Many years ago I first heard the term, woman's intuition. Intuition is another word for perception or keen insight. The Great Woman of Shunem was certainly perceptive and keen in her insight. Her husband was the head of the household, but she was the one with astute perception. The Hebrew word for perceive as it used there is; yada` (pronounced yaw-dah'); it means; to know (properly, to ascertain by seeing); observation, care, recognition. Once there was recognition, radical action was taken immediately. There are many women who possess discernment, but the Great Women get involved and are fearless when it is time to act on their discernment.

Consider this; holiness and the prophetic were passing by and she made sure the vessel came into her home to eat and be refreshed. Apostle Andre Cook, my mentor said: "As the level of her perception grew, so did the level of her giving." At first she constrained him to eat bread, but once in the house her giving went to another realm. Spiritual perception should always govern our giving and take it to higher heights. Giving should not be based on emotional manipulation or have any type of negative emotional attachment. Giving should not be rendered concomitant on what we may receive in return.

BUILT AND FULLY FURNISHED

Another great attribute that is clearly seen is that the Shunammite Woman was a woman of order and respect. Although she is a prosperous, powerful woman of influence in her community, she does not neglect to speak with her husband concerning blessing the holy man of God. She enlisted the help of her husband to accomplish her next level of blessing for the man of God. She told her husband: "Let us make a little chamber, I pray thee, on the wall; and let us set for him there a bed, and a table, and a stool, and a candlestick: and it shall be, when he cometh to us, that he shall turn in thither" (2 Kings 4:10). It wasn't enough for the holy prophetic presence to stop by occasionally to eat bread; she wanted it to abide in her home. She wanted to be connected to it so she was willing to make a radical move financially, positionally, and structurally to facilitate it. Can you imagine going from inviting someone into your house to eat, then deciding to put an addition on the house so the person can rest there? I call it the chazaq anointing or the chazaq blessing. It is an anointing or a grace for radical giving based on the ability of the giver not only to perceive that the individual in their midst is a holy man or woman of God, but to act on that perception.

During that time and in that culture the addition was built on the top of the house. What a marvelous picture of her house being covered by the Holy Prophetic Presence of God that flowed through His Prophet Elisha. With the aid of her husband, she built the chamber for the prophet and fully furnished it. I am certain it was furnished with the best she had to offer because that is what Great Women do; they operate in a spirit of excellence in whatever they put their hands to do. The more you read about her life, the more it will inspire you. Her kindness was not motivated by any hidden agenda, or to obtain recognition or even a special blessing, just a deep desire to be a blessing to Elisha.

When the prophet asked his servant Gehazi to call the woman and she stood by him. "And he said unto him, Say now unto her, Behold, thou hast been careful for us with all this care; what is to be done for thee? wouldest thou be spoken for to the king, or to the captain of the host? And she answered, I dwell among mine own people" (2 Kings 4:13). She didn't need government assistance because she was self-sufficient.

PROPHET OR 'PROFIT'?

The prophet was willing to speak to the king on her behalf, if she had a need. The prophets of old had the ear of kings; unlike the so called 'profits' of today. Elisha was willing to use his favor with the king to grant a special blessing to her, but she did not want anything in return for her generosity. The prophet was insistent because he understood the kingdom principle of the prophet's reward for someone who gave a prophet a glass of water. The Shunammite woman's reward would be great because she went way above a glass of water, for the prophet—she built an addition on her house. Great Women are not average or mediocre in giving. They are radical givers who give from a pure heart. The Bible instructs us not to forget to entertain strangers because some have entertained angels unawares by doing so. Elisha was not an angel, but he was a holy man of God who carried a heavy prophetic mantle. That mantle would release a proceeding word that would transform the Great Woman's life. There are some people who believe they can use money to earnestly seek and get a word from a prophet that will change the course of their life. The Great Woman of Shunem extended kindness to the man of God without expecting anything in return, and God honored her faithfulness. Giving liberally and generously without any agenda will cause blessings to come upon you.

There was something major that was missing from the Great Woman's life. Her wealth could not buy it and the king could not give it to her. Like the Great Woman, Hannah, the Shunammite woman had a barren womb. However, the prophet had a word in his belly that would take her from barren to fruitful. The authentic prophetic word has the ability to cause climatic changes as is recorded where Elijah told King Ahab that there would neither be dew nor rain these years but according to my word. The prophetic word has the ability to bring fertility, to bring life and resurrection to a barren, dead womb. When Gehazi told the prophet that the woman had no child and her husband was old, the man of God released a prophetic word of life to her when he stated emphatically: "About this season, according to the time of life, thou shalt embrace a son. And she said, Nay, my lord, thou man of God, do not lie unto thine handmaid. And the woman conceived, and bare a son at that season that Elisha had said unto her, according to the time of life" (2 Kings 4: 16-17).

Great Women know that barren areas of their lives do not diminish who they are. They do not allow singleness, a barren womb, a divorce, a rape or a molestation to stop them from manifesting the chazaq anointing. They know the proceeding word from God through the mouth of His prophet will cause the most barren place to become fruitful. In the life of the Great Woman of Shunem we see the manifestation of that principle. She thought the man of God had missed it when he told her she would embrace a son. It must have been inconceivable to her that after such a long time of being without child, God could perform the inconceivable, and she could give birth. I don't believe she was being disrespectful when she asked him not to lie to her. She had gone so long without a child, endured so much anguish, she may have thought giving birth would not be her portion in life. The potency of the prophetic word will overcome doubt and uncertainty. The prophetic word spoken to her by Elisha was fulfilled in its season. She birthed a son, but that birth brought a tragedy of such an immense proportion, it caused her greatness to go to another dimension. Elevation in God is accompanied by tests and trials but Great Women are able to pass them with flying colors.

STAY IN YOUR LANE

While out in the field with his father and the reapers her son complained about a pain in his head. His father's response was to tell someone to take him to his mother. Thank God for mothers; where would we be without them? Irrespective of the relationship some people have with their mother, she gave the precious gift of life and for that she should be celebrated as a Great Woman. The father realized his wife, the mother of his son would know what to do in that critical situation. He knew his lane, and he certainly knew hers. He helped to build the addition on the house for the man of God, but he knew when it was time for quick action, when his son's life was on the line, he had to get his son to his mother because she was the one with the spiritual perception.

When her son dies, sitting on her knees, she does not fall apart but springs into action. Greatness is molded and shaped in the furnace of affliction, not in the lap of luxury.

Adversity will either make a coward of us or it will motivate us to rise to greatness. The Shunammite woman did not wilt under the intense heat and pressure of the sudden death of her son; she sparkled like a precious diamond. She went up, and laid him on the bed of the man of God, and shut the door upon him, and went out.

IT SHALL BE WELL!

She knew exactly where to place her son's body. When she constrained the man of God to eat bread, she did not know he would speak a word in season to her inability to conceive. When the level of her giving increased, based on the increase in her level of perception, resulting in the building of a prophetic chamber on top of her house, she had no idea she would receive a miraculous blessing from God. She had no idea that she would conceive and birth a son, let alone that her son would die. She was unyielding in her belief that the same holy man of God who spoke the in season word to cause her barren womb to open and be fruitful, was able to speak a word to resurrect her son. 2 Kings 4:22-23 states,"And she called unto her husband, and said, Send me, I pray thee, one of the young men, and one of the asses, that I may run to the man of God, and come again. And he said, Wherefore wilt thou go to him to day? it is neither new moon, nor sabbath. And she said, It shall be well."

The test of true greatness is how one handles his or herself in the midst of a great tragedy. The death of a child is a tragedy of immense and epic proportion. The death of an only child whom you thought you could not have, only makes it more egregious. How many mothers could retain any semblance of self-composure in the face of death especially when it involved their children? Who can claim they would remain immovable, unshakable, seemingly undeterred in the midst of disaster, and not be left feeling helpless, overwrought, perhaps even screaming hysterically? That in itself defines the enduring, sterling qualities and attributes of a 'Great Woman'; of one who will put her faith and trust in the Lord God in the worst possible circumstances, regardless of what she sees, regardless of what she hears, or how she may feel.

Once again, we see the order and respect she operated in. Her response to her husband showed great poise. She does not usurp the authority of her husband or belittle him because of the spiritual dimension she walked in. She advised him that she needed to get to the man of God. Remember—he was the one who told one of the reapers to take the child to his mother when he was having the pain in his head.

Now she tells him she needs to get to the man of God, and he wants to engage her in a religious conversation about the fact that it was neither new moon nor Sabbath. Great Women are not shackled by religious tradition, but are steadfast and resolute to press beyond those limiting traditions to get to the holy prophetic presence, even when it is their husband who is stuck in religious tradition. She makes haste and does not argue, she does not panic, and she does not become abusive; she simply tells him,"it shall be well."

When you are dealing with a life and death situation and the people closest to you lack discernment, please do not lose your composure or allow their lack of understanding to discombobulate you. Just gather your thoughts and declare, "it shall be well." To his credit, her husband does not persist in his line of conversation, but allows her to go to the man of God. Blessed will be the man who learns to trust the Help Meet, the Good Thing, The Great Woman in his life. Some men would have wasted valuable time trying to make their point, some would have used a spirit of control to restrict her movement, but her husband knew the caliber of wife he was blessed with, so he held his peace when she said: "it shall be well." To my reader, I offer you the same words spoken by the Great Woman from Shunem in your time of crisis. Trust in the Lord Jesus Christ and know: "it shall be well."

SADDLE YOUR ASS

After speaking those four profound words to her husband, the Bible declares; "Then she saddled an ass, and said to her servant, Drive, and go forward; slack not thy riding for me, except I bid thee" (2 Kings 4:24). When your situation is critical, you cannot depend on someone else to saddle your ass; you better know how to do it yourself. And make sure you have some folks around you who know how to serve.When she got close to Mount Carmel the man of God saw her and sent his servant Gehazi to ask her three specific questions. Was it well with her; Was it well with her husband; Was it well with the child? Her response to Gehazi reveals even more about her greatness and her tenacious desire to get to the man of God. Remember, when her husband engaged her in a conversation about not being able to see the man of God because it was neither a new moon nor the Sabbath, she stayed calm, cool and collected when she told him: "It shall be well." Now, she has Gehazi in front of her asking her the questions as the man of God directed him and her discernment is still strong.

IT IS WELL!

The Shunammite Woman knew Gehazi was not the one she needed to be speaking with; he was not the holy man of God who was flowing in the heavy prophetic oil, so she told him; "it is well." The closer she came to the man of God, the stronger the word of faith she spoke. She went from, "it shall be well, to, "it is well." We must not allow religious tradition to block or stop us. We must not spend valuable time in long conversations with individuals who do not carry the holy prophetic oil. And when she came to the man of God upon the hill, she caught him by the feet, but Gehazi came near to thrust her away. The man of God told him, "Let her alone; for her soul is vexed within her: and the Lord hath hid it from me and hath not told me" (2 Kings 4:27). She has to climb a hill to get to the man of God, which speaks of the fact that we must overcome hurdles to get there. The hill represents a high place that holy prophetic men and women of God occupy. Religion tried to stop her and now an overzealous armor bearer wants to get physical with her, but there is a reason why she is called a Great Woman. Her veneer was so calm during the crisis, the prophet could not discern the immensity of the tragedy she was dealing with. You must be able to hold your peace and suppress any negative emotions during the most violent storm and trust that by the grace of God, "it shall be, and it is well." Gehazi tried to thrust her away; no wonder she did not spend valuable time engaged in conversation with him.

Her perception that allowed her to recognize the holiness in Elisha also allowed her to discern his servant Gehazi. She is a 'Great Woman' she is humble enough to stoop to the man of God's feet. "... How beautiful are the feet of them that preach the gospel of peace, and bring glad tidings of good things" (Romans 10:15).

In a moment of transparency, she said, "Did I desire a son of my lord? Did I not say, Do not deceive me? Then he said to Gehazi, Gird up thy loins, and take my staff in thine hand, and go thy way: if thou meet any man, salute him not; and if any salute thee, answer him not again: and lay my staff upon the face of the child. And the mother of the child said, As the Lord liveth, and as thy soul liveth, I will not leave thee. And he arose, and followed her" (2 Kings 4: 28-30). She was not going to leave the man of God because she knew he was the one who had the power and authority from the Lord to raise her son from the dead. When you encounter a true holy man or woman of God, don't leave their presence until you receive everything the Lord has given them for you.

The man of God sent his servant with the staff and instructions on what to do, but the Great Woman's perception let her know to stay with the man of God; and she was right. Gehazi was not able to raise the child. He had the man of God's staff, but he did not have his anointing. Men and women of God, there are some assignments you will not be able to delegate to your staff; you have to handle them yourselves. The anointing is not in your staff, it is in you. When the man of God went to the house, the spirit of death had to leave because death could not dwell in the place the 'Great Woman' had built for the holy man of God.

The nonplused response of the Shunammite woman in a moment of crisis coined and immortalized the phrases, "It shall be well and it is well" and is synonymous with the scripture verse found in Romans 4:17— "... even God, who quickeneth the dead, and calleth those things which be not as though they were". There was nothing at all well with the Shunammite woman when she spoke both the future and present tense of her state of being. Her world as she knew it had drastically changed; her heart must have been breaking to realize that her only son was now dead. How very admirable and quite astonishing that this 'Great Woman' never once vocalized in the form of a negative report or a verbal confession declaring that her child was no longer alive. The words "my son is dead" never proceeded out of her mouth and it was her faith that grounded her, sustained her, comforted her, and gave her the rationale to know exactly what to do. Her faith allowed her to believe in the impossible, to believe in the supernatural. Her monumental faith in God separates the Shunammite woman as that rarefied gem; sets her apart from other women in the Bible; earns her a rightful induction into the Hall of Faith; and earns her the extraordinary, unmatched status as a 'Great Woman'. Her unwavering faith is her most outstanding, prized, intangible asset given to her descendants and to all who read her story. She did not have a single doubt or negative thought pertaining to her son's life; she knew the Spirt of God operating through His prophet, had the capacity to quicken her son from the dead as easily as he had quickened her womb to give him life.

In addition to her unparalleled faith in God, it was her staunch belief in His promises that are irreversible. It was the prophet's word from the very oracles of God spoken over her, that is immutable; it was the delivery of a very special blessing of a son from God which was an unspoken desire in her heart; and it was her ready expectation that God would be able to perform a miracle by resurrecting her son, that superseded all logic and reasoning to the contrary.

May we all be divinely inspired, and equally possess the Shunammite woman's level of faith so that we can gain in courage, trust in God, focus on His word, and on His promises despite seemingly dead matters; despite adverse circumstances;and despite evil and negative reports. We can live by the testimony and creed of the Shunammite woman by applying, following, and leading by example, from one whose spiritual legacy of a 'Great Woman', one who had no name, is to this day imparting undeniable faith, and impacting innumerable lives, long after her death.

In actuality, no name is needed for the Shunammite woman because long after a person is dead and buried their name may not be remembered, it might even be forgotten. However, there is something that will live on forever, and forever be imprinted on the hearts and minds of those close to the dearly departed; something memorable, something valuable; something enduring that is passed down from generation to generation. Something that moth and rust cannot corrupt and thieves cannot break in and steal. It is a living legacy that keeps on giving. Although prosperous and highly positioned, there was something much more than a financial legacy, and much more than material assets that her son stood to inherit.

The Shunammite woman left a lasting legacy; an endowment of kindness, consideration, generosity, and hospitality. She was a gracious ministering servant toward her fellow man, investing in the Kingdom of God, in God's holy men, and amassing intangible assets that were heavenly treasures that money could never purchase and were considered priceless in God's divine treasury. Her descendants could be very proud of the Shunammite woman because she has been immortalized and highly exalted in the indestructible, infinite, and immutable word of God. There are many wealthy individuals who are rich beyond imagination, and yet they are spiritually impoverished because they did nothing to finance the Kingdom of God, nor did they seek the Kingdom of God and His righteousness. The word of God says in Mark 8:36 (NIV): "What good is it for someone to gain the whole world, yet forfeit their soul?"

Which brings to mind the question; what kind of lasting legacy will you leave your descendants? Will you leave more than a financial legacy? Will you leave a rich spiritual legacy? Will you leave a legacy of upstanding moral principles?A legacy of the riches of God's glory in the name of our Lord, Jesus Christ, that your descendants can pass down from generation to generation, adding spiritual wealth, and spiritual enrichment to many lives including your own?

DISTINCT QUALITIES OF GREATNESS

- Bold
- Keen Discernment
- Builder/Facilitator
- Radical Giver
- Not a Usurper of Authority
- Poised in the Midst of Pressure
- Refused to Be Distracted
- Favor From the King
- Ability to Endure

Huldah

One Who Lacks Courage to Start, Has Already Finished

HULDAH—THE PROPHETIC AWAKENING

If we are going to see real development in the world, then our best investment is WOMEN. —Desmond Tutu

Huldah resided in that part of Jerusalem called the Mishneh, or the college, which was a suburb of Jerusalem. She was held in such veneration that Jewish writers say she and Jehoiada the priest were the only persons not of the house of David (2 Chronicles 24:16) who were ever buried in Jerusalem. She is one of three women in the Old Testament who had the distinction of the title of prophetess conferred upon them. The word is used in Isaiah 8:3 to describe Isaiah's wife, but it is conferred upon her because she is the prophet's wife. In an online article on the website jaw.org titled: "Huldah, the Prophet: Midrash and Aggadah" by Tamar Kadari. The author writes: "Huldah is one of the seven women prophets of Israel enumerated by the Rabbis: Sarah, Miriam, Deborah, Hannah, Abigail, Huldah and Esther (BT Megillah 14a); she is also mentioned among the twenty-three truly upright and righteous women who came forth from Israel" (Midrash Tadshe, Ozar ha-Midrashim [Eisenstein], p. 474).

Huldah does not have the name recognition of Miriam or Deborah, but she was used mightily of God like they were. That tells me that a person does not have to be famous or well known in order to do great exploits for God. Some of you may not know who you are, but the important thing is that you are known by the Almighty God, the Creator of the heavens and the earth.

Huldah does not have a lot of recorded words in the Bible but when she spoke, her words triggered revival. Great Women know it is not the amount of words they speak, but the impact their words have when they open their mouths and allow Jesus to speak through them. To understand her greatness and the impact of her prophetic ministry, we must look at the action King Josiah took after his emissaries returned with a word from Huldah. Josiah was the great grandson of King Hezekiah. His grandfather and his father were exceptionally wicked, but he was used by God to usher in spiritual reform. Josiah was eight years old when his reign began. He came to the throne at a young age, so he must have had godly people around him to mentor and tutor him. Eight is the number of new beginnings and his ascent to the throne ushered in a new beginning for the nation.

In the eighteenth year of his reign, Josiah sent his scribe to the house of the Lord and to the high priest to check the silver in the treasury. Silver was given to the 'doers' of the work so they could repair the breaches. King Josiah was young, but he was mature; he had a heart that was dedicated to the Lord and to His house. He had a mind to repair the breach in the house of the Lord; a breach caused by years of cavalier neglect. The high priest gave Josiah's scribe the book of the law to be delivered to the king. When it was read Josiah rent his clothes because he realized how far the people had strayed away from God. It was a realization which prompted him to take immediate action. He told his emissaries, "Go ye, enquire of the Lord for me, and for the people, and for all Judah, concerning the words of this book that is found: for great is the wrath of the Lord that is kindled against us, because our fathers have not hearkened unto the words of this book, to do according unto all that which is written concerning us" (2 Kings 22:13). I love the fact that his desire was to inquire of the Lord first. His concern was not only for himself, but for all the people of Judah. He did not sugar-coat the gravity of the nation's backslidden condition, and the response of the Lord that he knew was inevitable.

Josiah sent five emissaries to Jerusalem and they communed with the Great Woman, Prophetess Huldah, as she released the word of the Lord to them for the king. Josiah was no chauvinist; he knew Huldah flowed in the prophetic oil and he was humble enough to inquire of the Lord through her. In that time and season prophets and prophetesses ministered to kings, instructing them and giving them direction for the nation and for their personal lives. The Jamieson Fausset & Brown Commentary has this to say: "The occasion was urgent, and therefore they were sent, not to Zephaniah--(Zeph 1:1), who was perhaps young, nor to Jeremiah, who was probably absent from his house in Anathoth, but to one who was at hand, and known for her prophetic gifts--to Huldah, who was probably at this time a widow." Her husband Shallum, was grandson of one Harhas, "keeper for you of the wardrobe." If this means the priestly wardrobe, he must have been a Levite. But it probably refers to the royal wardrobe.

THE TRUTH, THE WHOLE TRUTH, AND NOTHING BUT THE TRUTH

When Huldah opened her mouth, and released the word of the Lord to Josiah's emissaries, she did not give them a soul soothing word to comfort their flesh inorder to get a monetary offering, like some of the modern-day 'profits'.

She released the word of the Lord with power and authority when she said: "Thus saith the Lord God of Israel, Tell the man that sent you to me, Thus saith the Lord, Behold, I will bring evil upon this place, and upon the inhabitants thereof, even all the words of the book which the king of Judah hath read." (2 Kings 22:15-16). You do not need prophets speaking to you out of their flesh or out of their soul; you need a true prophet of God who is willing to speak, the truth, the whole truth and nothing but the truth. You need a prophet who is willing to speak the word given to him or her by the Lord for you, even if it is a hard word. Great Women like Huldah have that type of Prophetic Pedigree.

Huldah went on to tell the emissaries, "Because they have forsaken me, and have burned incense unto other gods, that they might provoke me to anger with all the works of their hands. Therefore, my wrath shall be kindled against this place, and shall not be quenched." (verse 17). Judgment was coming to the nation and it is not easy when God sends you to release a word of a coming judgment, but when He does, His messengers must be obedient. The prophets of old always came to the people with a two-fold word from the Lord: a warning of a coming judgment, but also a word of hope and reconciliation if they were willing to repent. God spoke these words to one of those prophets by the name of Ezekiel: "Son of man, I have made thee a watchman unto the house of Israel therefore hear the word at my mouth, and give them warning from me. When I say unto the wicked, Thou shalt surely die; and thou givest him not warning, nor speakest to warn the wicked from his wicked way, to save his life; the same wicked man shall die in his iniquity; but his blood will I require at thine hand. Yet if thou warn the wicked, and he turn not from his wickedness, nor from his wicked way, he shall die in his iniquity; but thou hast delivered thy soul" (Ezekiel 3:17-19).

The nation received a word of impending judgment but Josiah received a comforting word because his heart was tender before the Lord. Huldah told the emissaries: "But to the king of Judah which sent you to inquire of the Lord, thus shall ye say to him, Thus saith the Lord God of Israel. As touching the words which thou hast heard; Because thine heart was tender, and thou hast humbled thyself before the Lord, when thou heardest what I spake against this place, and against the inhabitants thereof, that they should become a desolation and a curse, and hast rent thy clothes, and wept before me; I also have heard thee, saith the Lord. Behold therefore, I will gather thee unto thy fathers, and thou shalt be gathered into thy grave in peace; and thine eyes shall not see all the evil which I will bring upon this place.

And they brought the king word again." (verses 18-20). The word from the Lord to Josiah through Huldah sheds light on the kind of person he was. He had a tender heart; he humbled himself before the Lord; he rent his clothes; and he wept before the Lord. He was a humble king and a man greatly committed to the word of the Lord. God hears and answers the prayers of the humble.

When you seek the Lord for the welfare and benefit of others, He will not leave your business unattended. Based on the prophetic word he received from Huldah, King Josiah gathered unto him all the elders of Judah and Jerusalem, as well as the priests, the prophets and all the people. Great and small were assembled with him. The bona fide prophetic word always points people in a godly direction, even if it is a word of judgment. A word of judgment comes to let them know they need to repent. What kind of word are people hearing when you open your mouth? Gossip, backbiting, cursing? Great Women do not slander people; they speak words that point people to God. Proverbs 18:21 states, "Death and life are in the power of the tongue: and they that love it shall eat the fruit thereof." How are people being affected by the words coming from your mouth? Are they being convicted to turn their hearts back to God? Are they receiving comfort from you, or are they receiving criticism? Prophetess Huldah's words triggered something in young King Josiah that caused him to make a radical move.

"And the king stood by a pillar, and made a covenant before the Lord, to walk after the Lord, and to keep his commandments and his testimonies and his statutes with all their heart and all their soul, to perform the words of this covenant that were written in this book. And all the people stood to the covenant" (2 Kings 23:3). I am in awe of the power of the proceeding word of God that comes out of the mouth of His prophetic vessels. As previously stated, Huldah does not have the name recognition of some of the other prophets of the Bible, but her prophetic ministry was so dynamic in God, it shifted the nation. God is no respecter of persons; please get this word in your spirit and understand you have the potential to be great in God and to do great things for God, like Huldah, like Josiah, irrespective of your age, your gender, or any external factor. When you yield your will to the Lord and keep your heart tender before Him; when you are willing to cry out to Him in prayer; He will turn stumbling blocks into stepping stones. Like Prophetess Huldah and other Great Women, God will use you to impact nations, and to bring restoration and transformation.

WOMAN THOU ART LOOSED—LOOSED FOR GOD'S GREATNESS

I have a conference line that I use for teaching on Thursday nights and for several months, I taught on the topics "The Ministry of Women" and "Great Women." The Holy Spirit reminded me of a time when I spoke with a woman of God who referred to the paradigm shifting book written, and the conference convened by Bishop TD Jakes, entitled: "Woman Thou Art Loosed." The question that came to my mind when she mentioned it was, "Loosed from what, to do what?" The answer that came to me was loosed from any and everything that hinders or stifles your God-given ability to manifest GREATNESS! Memories of rape, being cheated on, and molestation will not hinder you, they will not scar you and cause you to be mentally and emotionally crippled. God did not loose you from the bondage of sin and empower you with the precious gift of Holy Spirit to leave you in a proverbial no man's land of idleness. When He brings you out of one place or state it is for the sole purpose of bringing you into something or some place greater. One of my often-quoted scriptures is, "Now unto him that is able to do exceeding abundantly above all that we ask or think, according to the power that worketh in us" (Ephesians 3:20).

When I ministered this word on the PDIC (Prophetic Destiny Impact Call), the Holy Spirit had me to utter a prophetic declaration to the listeners and I release that declaration to you my readers! I prophesy to the Daughters of Zion; King Jesus has loosed you to fulfill your prophetic destiny:

- Loosed you from poverty into prosperity
- Loosed you from depression into the joy of the Lord
- Loosed you from sickness, disease and infirmity into good health
- Loosed you from mediocrity into GREATNESS
- Loosed you from every form of bondage into freedom

DISTINCT QUALITIES OF GREATNESS

- Trustworthy
- Speaks with Authority
- Not Intimidated
- Did Not Allow Gender to Box Her in
- Prophetic Utterances Facilitated a Reform
- Not Afraid to Speak Out Against Idolatry and Wickedness
- Others Took Actions When She Spoke
- A Clear and Concise Female Prophetic Voice in a Male Dominated Society
- Assertive

Section Five

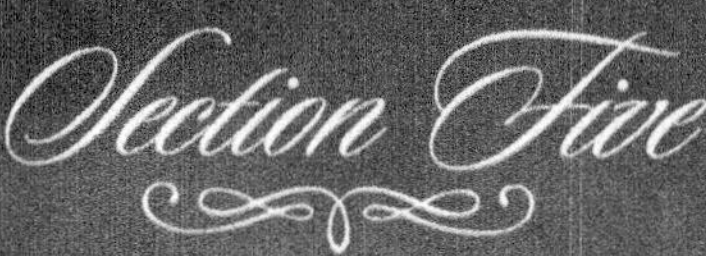

Precious Jewels
DIAMONDS IN THE ROUGH

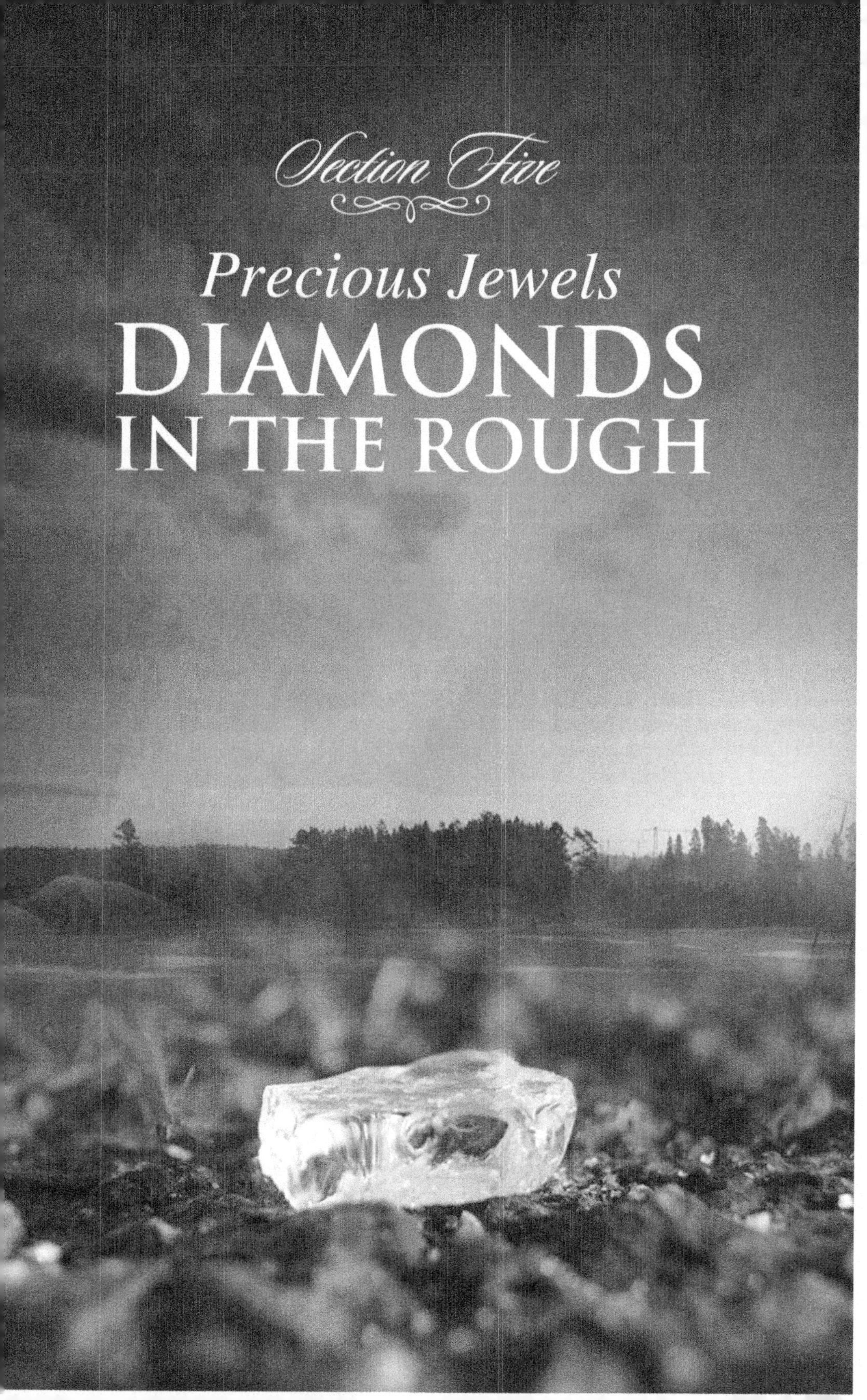

The Little Maid

The Little Maid: Purpose Personified; No bees, No Honey; No Work, No Money

THE LITTLE MAID—POSITIONED FOR DIVINE PURPOSE

uccess isn't about how much money you make—it's about the difference you make in people's lives. —Michelle Obama

The Bible declares, the steps of the righteous are ordered by the Lord; that declaration does not mean those steps always take us to places that are comfortable. God has no problem taking His people through wildernesses and deserts to accomplish His purpose. The children of God who learn to trust Him in those difficult places, the ones who refuse to murmur, complain, or look back to Egypt, will know God in a greater dimension and do exploits for Him. God spoke these words to His people Israel, "Behold, I have refined thee, but not with silver; I have chosen thee in the furnace of affliction" (Isaiah 48:10).

The Great Woman who is my subject for this chapter is not named in the Bible. She does not have a lofty position; she has a menial one. She is referred to as a little maid, but she is strategically positioned by God to speak words that are a catalyst for one of the great miracles performed in the Bible. I remember years ago when my wife worked in the home of a prominent man and woman of God taking care of one of their adopted children, and when the position became hectic for her she resigned from it. I was so inspired by the story of the little maid, and what she was used by God to accomplish in the life of a great man, that I told my wife God was going to send her back to the couple's home because her assignment was not finished. Not long after I spoke with her, the lady of the house asked her if she could come back and she agreed.

I won't keep you in suspense any longer as to the identity of the little maid, the Great Woman of consideration for this chapter. Her story is found in 2 Kings 5, which records the story of the healing of Naaman the leper. Naaman was a very accomplished individual who was not of the commonwealth of Israel, but He was used to fulfill the divine purpose of God. I refer to his list of accomplishments recorded in the Bible as his resume, or as the British say, his curriculum vitae. He is described as captain of the host of the king of Syria, a great man with his master, and honorable because the Lord had given deliverance unto Syria. He was also a mighty man in valour. When I teach or preach this story of the little maid, and how she was used in Naaman's life, I mention the fact that his resume was interrupted by a conjunction which introduces a new thought or idea.

The conjunction which interrupts his illustrious resume is the three letter word `but'. The words that follow`but' cast an ominous cloud over all his accomplishments— "he was a leper." Leprosy was a dreaded incurable disease at that time.

The Bible describes leprosy as a plague in Leviticus 13:3-4, "And the priest shall look on the plague in the skin of the flesh: and when the hair in the plague is turned white, and the plague in sight be deeper than the skin of his flesh, it is a plague of leprosy: and the priest shall look on him, and pronounce him unclean. If the bright spot be white in the skin of his flesh, and in sight be not deeper that the skin, and the hair thereof be not turned white; then the priest shall shut up him that hath the plague seven days." God gave Moses specific instructions how it should be dealt with. The person with the leprosy had to be quarantined because it was contagious. As long as the condition persisted the individual had to be separated from the congregation. Naaman was from Syria so the laws given to Moses by God did not apply to him, and it does not appear that the leprosy had reached a stage where he had to be quarantined and could not fulfill his duties as a military leader. Naaman needed a miracle and that miracle was not something he could get from Rimmon the god of the Syrians. The catalyst for his miracle would come from an unlikely source; the little maid. God specializes in using unlikely sources for His Glory and Honor.

THE HEART OF THE MATTER IS: IT'S A MATTER OF THE HEART

The little maid was captured from her beloved nation, taken to enemy territory, and placed in the house of a leper to be his wife's maid. The first, and only time that she speaks and her words are recorded in the Bible is not about herself or her condition. Her greatness is evidenced by the words that emanated from her mouth. Those words are a reflection of what was in her heart because Jesus declared, "A good man out of the good treasure of his heart bringeth forth that which is good; and an evil man out of the evil treasure of his heart bringeth forth that which is evil: for of the abundance of the heart his mouth speaketh" (Luke 6:45). The little maid did not allow the captivity and the separation from her homeland to cause the root of bitterness to permeate and saturate her heart, and cause her speech to become bitter and toxic. Instead of speaking about her situation, when she opened her mouth she spoke to Naaman's condition. "And she said unto her mistress, Would God my lord were with the prophet that is in Samaria! For he would recover him of his leprosy" (2 Kings 5:3).

The writer placed an exclamation point after the word Samaria for emphasis. Although she is a captive in the house, and her position would be considered a menial one—she does not lose respect for Naaman, but calls him lord. She must have lived an exemplary life in the house of Naaman as her words set in motion a chain of events that led him to the prophet of God. Her words were held in such high esteem that someone took them to Naaman and informed him of what the little maid from Israel had said concerning him.

If you are currently dealing with a situation that is holding you captive—what kind of words are you allowing to come out of your mouth? The words from your mouth are a reflection of the condition of your heart. Are they words of life or words of death? Death and life are in the power of the tongue and words can destruct or they can construct. Have you allowed the things you are dealing with to cause a root of bitterness to seize your heart, resulting in your words being toxic? Or, are you able to rise above the condition and the environment and speak life to those around you? Psalms 19:14 states, "Let the words of my mouth, and the meditation of my heart, be acceptable in thy sight, O Lord, my strength, and my redeemer." Great Women are careful to guard their hearts against bitterness, because they know the issues of life flow out of it. The strength they draw from their Redeemer keeps their hearts strong and fortified against anger, bitterness, and un-forgiveness.

When I first read the little maid's story I wondered why Naaman, his wife, the king, or anyone in Syria would think that the prophet of Samaria could help when God had given Syria victory over Israel? I would assume Naaman would have thought; God had forsaken them. The Syrians may have believed it was their god who had given them mastery over Israel. The key is the lifestyle lived by the little maid that gave her words credence and credibility. In the midst of the most egregious environments, Great Women maintain their integrity, their love walk, and their peace.

God expects you to maintain your integrity, love walk, and peace in the midst of a difficult environment, so He can bring deliverance to others through you. What you are dealing with at the present time is not solely about you, but about what God wants to do in and through you. He wants to use your misery as a platform to launch your ministry. Humble yourself like the little maid and allow God to manifest a great work through you.

The little maid's words were so important they reached the ears of the king of Syria and he took action. God can use your words to cause kings and leaders in prominent positions to take action, if you allow Him to be Lord in your situation. If you allow the situation to cause bitterness in your heart, the words coming out of your mouth will be used by the adversary to cause devastation. The little maid was confident that God would work through His prophet in Samaria to bring healing to Naaman, and she stated that emphatically. Do not allow your condition to cause fear to supersede faith. God's power and ability are not diminishedbecause He has you in a waiting room of preparation for a divine assignment. I do not believe the little maid was in Naaman's home by chance or happenstance, but by divine appointment. Do not assume that divine appointments will always take you to comfortable places. Do not allow the difficulty of the place or position you currently occupy to distract you and cause you to miss an opportunity to fulfill God's assignment. Great Women have the ability to exercise great focus when the pressure is rising.

Once her words were told to the king, he said—Go and visit the prophet, go, and I will send a letter unto the king of Israel. When Naaman departed Syria to go to the land of Israel, he did not do so empty handed. He took with him ten talents of silver, and six thousand pieces of gold, and ten changes of raiment. Obviously, he was serious about meeting with the prophet of God. When the king of Israel received the letter sent to him by the king of Syria requesting healing for his servant Naaman, his immediate distress was evident. Juxtaposition means, to place things together in-order to compare or to see the contrasting effect. The king of Israel had power, authority and wealth; the little maid had faith in God and his prophet. Juxtapose the words spoken by the maid and the words spoken by the king of Israel when he received the letter, and you will see further evidence of the little maid's greatness.

"And it came to pass, when the king of Israel had read the letter, that he rent his clothes, and said, Am I God, to kill and to make alive, that this man doth send unto me to recover a man of his leprosy? wherefore consider, I pray you, and see how he seeketh a quarrel against me" (2 Kings 5:7). Astonishingly, the king has an opportunity to demonstrate to the heathen king of Syria, the power and authority of His God, but instead of rising to the occasion, he allows fear to take hold of him and begins to speak negatively. The maid's words set the stage for a great miracle, but her king's fear and doubt was trying to destroy it. All was not lost, because the prophet Elisha heard that the king had rent his clothes, so he took action.

When he heard what the king did he spoke emphatically, just like the little maid. Elisha sent these words to the king of Israel, "... Wherefore hast thou rent thy clothes? let him come now to me, and he shall know that there is a prophet in Israel" (verse 8). Reader, you must have confidence in the prophetic word God has placed in your belly. When people in greater, more powerful, and more prestigious positions than you are doubtful, cast not away your confidence in your God because it has great recompense of reward. Elisha was bold and confident in his God like his spiritual father and mentor, the Prophet Elijah. Elisha knew the story of Elijah standing before king Ahab and telling him, "... As the Lord God of Israel liveth, before whom I stand, there shall not be dew nor rain these years, but according to my word" (1 Kings 17:1).

Great Women speak the word of the Lord with authority, boldness, and confidence. Reader, you have the word of faith in your mouth and in your heart; please do not hesitate to use it. The prophet Jeremiah was told by God that He hastens His word to perform it. The little maid must have grown up hearing about the exploits God did through His people, especially His prophets. She refused to allow the captivity and the menial position in the house of Naaman to shake her confidence in her God and in His prophet. She was not intimated or fearful of the condition of Naaman because she knew that a connection with the prophet of God would secure his healing. Your words of faith are not limited to time and space like your physical body. You may be confined to a prison, a wheelchair, a hospital bed or a physically debilitating condition, but if you can maintain and speak the word of faith, you can bring transformation, not only to yourself, but to people in distant lands. Just like the little maid, there is power in your mouth; power to heal, power to deliver, and power to set the captives free.

The Bible is replete with examples of individuals who spoke words of faith that were the catalyst for healing and restoration. The gospel of Matthew records a story of a centurion coming to Jesus when He came into Capernaum, beseeching Him, and saying, "Lord, my servant lieth at home sick of the palsy, grievously tormented." His servant was at home paralyzed, but he had faith to believe that Jesus could heal him. He did not allow the fact that he was a Roman centurion to stop him from coming to Jesus. Faith, when it is applied, will lift us above earthly obstacles and hindrances. Jesus told him that He would come and heal him. The centurion's response caused Jesus to marvel at the type of faith he expressed. The centurion answered and said, "Lord, I am not worthy that thou shouldest come under my roof: but speak the word only, and my servant shall be healed. For I am a man under authority, having soldiers under me: and I say to this man, Go, and he goeth; and to another, Come, and he cometh; and to my servant, Do this, and he doeth it. When Jesus heard it, He marveled, and said to them that followed, Verily I say unto you, I have not found so great faith, no, not in Israel. Jesus went on to say to him, Go thy way; and as thou hast believed; so be it done unto thee. And his servant was healed in the selfsame hour" (Matthew 8:5-10, 13).

Times and seasons may change; people, places and things may change; but the word of the Lord is sealed forever. The centurion and the little maid were different people living in different times, but both understood the power of the spoken word. When Naaman came to meet Prophet Elisha, the prophet did not come out to meet him to bring attention to himself. He sent a messenger to Naaman with explicit instructions; "Go and wash in Jordan seven times, and thy flesh shall come again to thee, and thou shalt be clean" (2 Kings 5:10). Naaman almost allowed pride to block his miraculous healing. He was wroth because he thought Elisha would come out to him, stand, and call on the name of the Lord his God, and strike his hand over the place, and recover the leper. He did not understand that it was not about a religion; it was all about the power of the prophetic word. Eventually he came to his senses and listened to the servants who told him: "My father, if the prophet had bid thee do some great thing, wouldest thou not have done it? how much rather then, when he saith to thee, Wash, and be clean" (2 Kings 5:13)? When he humbled himself and obeyed the prophetic instructions, his flesh came again like unto the flesh of a little child, and he was clean.

The story in 2 Kings 5 includes many dignitaries; The king of Israel, the king of Syria, Naaman the great, honorable man of valour, Naaman's wife and the anointed prophet of God, Elisha. Naaman's healing from leprosy is one of the awesome miracles of the Bible. It blesses my heart to know the person used by God to start the process was the unsung 'Shero' who is nameless in the story. We are given her title and her position, which were not prestigious, but her words proved that she was positioned to fulfill divine purpose. She did not have to leave the house to effect change. Her words were powerful enough to travel to the ears of individuals of power and authority like Naaman, his wife, the king of Syria, and the king of Israel.

I take this opportunity to speak directly to you, my reader. You may find yourself in a menial place or position currently;

be encouraged and keep trusting in God. He can use you mightily in that place and position. Be sensitive to the leading of the Holy Spirit and hear what He is speaking to you. When He speaks, be bold enough to speak as He instructs and your words will effect transformation, just like the words of the Great Woman, known as the little maid.

READER, ARE YOU SAVED?

If you are reading this book and you have not confessed Jesus Christ as Savior and Lord of your life, please take this very important moment and place your hands over your heart and repeat these simple but powerful words to the Lord Jesus Christ. "Lord, I repent of my sins and I choose to turn from my sinful ways to your life transforming ways. I confess with my mouth and believe in my heart that you are the Son of God Who died for my sins and arose from the grave to give me eternal life." Glory to the name of Jesus Christ! You are saved. You are in right standing and in relationship with Jesus Christ. Continue to take time to praise and thank Him for His mercy and grace over your life. Now pray to find a church and pastor who ministers and teaches in the fullness of the Spirit of the Living God; like the little maid, allow your position to be used by God for His Divine Purpose!

Distinct Qualities of Greatness

- Meek and Mild Mannered
- Words are Transformational
- Fulfilled Divine Purpose
- Well Respected
- Did Not Allow Her Menial Position to Cloud Her Judgment
- Able to Operate Outside Her Comfort Zone
- Circumstance Did Not Make her Bitter; It Made Her Better
- She Rose to the Occasion
- Youthful Exuberance

Mary

Hail Mary: "Her Children Arise Up, And Call Her Blessed; Her Husband Also, And He Praiseth Her" (Proverbs 31:28)

MARY—BLESSED AND HIGHLY FAVORED

Nothing is impossible-the word itself says I'm possible.
—Audrey Hepburn

Years ago, while watching either a football game or listening to a game recap, I heard the term Hail Mary. I learned, a Hail Mary pass is a very long forward pass in American football, made in desperation with only a small chance of success. I am using the term in this chapter, not in the context of football, but to reference the greatest woman mentioned in the Bible. The word 'Hail' was used by the angel Gabriel in his salutation to Mary when he came to announce the conception of the Holy Child, Jesus. She is so venerated by the Catholic Church, a prayer is modeled by Catholics after the salutation given to her by Gabriel. Although I consider Mary the greatest woman in the Bible, I see no precedence for prayer in her name and worship of her. Nowhere in the Bible does she exalt herself, or is exalted by Jesus because she is His mother. I am led to believe that the basis of her veneration by the Catholic Church is grounded in traditions and scriptures not included in Bibles used by Protestants.

CAN ANYTHING GOOD COME OUT OF NAZARETH?

I consider Mary the greatest of all the women in the Bible because she was chosen by God to birth His Son, the Messiah. There were Great Women in the Bible who gave birth to sons and daughters who did exploits for the Kingdom of God, but Mary was the greatest because her Son was God robed in human flesh. She was a virgin at the time, so the conception is referred to as, The Immaculate Conception. Prior to conceiving the Messiah, Mary did not have much notoriety. She was from a city in Galilee named Nazareth, which had a bad reputation. It was remote from Jerusalem which was the center of Jewish life and worship. The city was located on a major trade route, and it was frequented by Gentile merchants and Roman soldiers. For these reasons the city's reputation was tarnished among the Jews. Jesus was born in Bethlehem in fulfillment of prophecy, but He grew up in Nazareth. Another example of the negative reputation Nazareth had, was encapsulated in the response Nathaniel gave when Philip told him, "We have found him, of whom Moses in the law, and the prophets, did write, Jesus of Nazareth, the son of Joseph" (John 1:45). Although Philip told him Jesus was the one written about by Moses in the law and the prophets, he could not wrap his mind around that revelation because he heard Jesus was from Nazareth. His response gives credence to that assertion. "And Nathanael said unto him, Can there any good thing come out of Nazareth? Philip saith unto him, Come and see" (John 1:46). Shallow people judge others based on external factors such as the color of their skin, the neighborhood they grew up in, and whether or not they received a good education. The Body of Christ is not void of these prejudices. Some Christians judge others based on their denomination, whether or not they speak in tongues, or whether or not they were baptized in Jesus' name or Father, Son and Holy Ghost. God is just, and is neither biased nor prejudiced as some people are.

In His infinite wisdom, the Almighty God chose a young, poor female from the ghetto to be the mother of His only begotten Son. I would like to think He did it so those living on the margins or the fringes of society would know: He is no respecter of persons. He didn't choose someone from a royal family to conceive and birth His Son. He didn't choose someone wealthy and highly educated. When His Son was born, He did not spend His first night in a palace dressed in clothing fit for a king. He spent His first night in a manger dressed in swaddling clothes. You have no control over how you came into this world, but what you can control is the choices you make while you are in this world.

I can only imagine what it was like for the young virgin when the angel Gabriel showed up and said, "Hail, thou that art highly favoured, the Lord is with thee: blessed art thou among women" (Luke 1:28). What a greeting, what a salutation for the young virgin to receive! Seeing the angel Gabriel must have represented a life transforming moment, but to hear him say, "Thou art highly favoured, the Lord is with thee: blessed art thou among women." She may have thought in her mind, who me? In many instances when God sends a word to someone chosen for a divine assignment, that word challenges the individual to do, or to be greater than his or her perceived capability. The word may appear to contradict the place or state where the individual is; it is much farther than their minds could ever conceive. It represents where God is taking them, and what He will do in and through them. Do not allow your current state or place to negate or cause you to doubt the place God is taking you, and the great things He will do in and through you. God's word concerning your destiny must take precedence and have preeminence over the limitations you experience in the natural.

Like Mary, Gideon had a divine visitation from the Lord. When the angel of the Lord came to him, he was threshing wheat by the winepress in order to hide from the Midianites. When the angel appeared to him, he said, The Lord is with thee, thou mighty man of valour. Gideon might have had a similar experience to Mary's. He did not feel like the Lord was with him and he certainly did not feel like a mighty man of valour. He didn't praise God for what the angel declared to him; on the contrary, he questioned the veracity of the message. He asked the angel how they could be in their present position if the Lord was with them, and where were all the miracles told to them by their fathers. When the Lord told him to go in his might because He was sending him to deliver Israel out of the hands of the Midianites, he responded: Oh my Lord, wherewith shall I save Israel? Behold, my family is poor in Manasseh, and I am the least in my father's house (Judges 6:15). Gideon was about to experience an even greater miracle than those told to them by their fathers, but he couldn't conceive it. Excuses will keep you average; God wants the extraordinary out of your life.

It takes faith to believe the word of God when the circumstance is screaming something else. God says you are healed, but your body is wracked in pain from a disease the doctor said is incurable. Whose report are you going to believe, the medical report, or the report of the Lord? God said He is going to open the prison door. Whose report are you going to believe, the righteous Judge of the whole earth who sits high and looks low, or the earthly judge? Man can say what they think will happen based on probability, but God determines what actually happens, even when the situation has the look and feel of impossibility.

Great Women go by what God says and not what their situation says. After all, God has the ability to call those things that be not as though they are. When God calls something it has to line up with what He calls it, no matter how impossible it looks. When the earth was without form and void, God said, let there be light. When He spoke, darkness had to give way to light. The apostle Paul told the Corinthians, "For God, who commanded the light to shine out of darkness, hath shined in our hearts, to give the light of the knowledge of the glory of God in the face of Jesus Christ. But we have this treasure in earthen vessels, that the excellency of the power may be of God, and not of us" (2 Corinthians 4:6-7). The vessel represents your life. A life that may seem fragile and breakable, but there is a light, a treasure inside of you and you must let it shine. That is why Jesus called you the light of the world.

All of us have some dark areas in our lives, but it is important to remember that God commanded the light to shine out of darkness. Do not allow dark thoughts to inveigle you to do dark deeds. When darkness attempts to overtake you, turn on the light.

Mary may not have felt blessed living in Nazareth, she probably wondered like Gideon, if the Lord was with her why was she in that place? We have all had similar thoughts at one time or another. Mary was perplexed by the salutation because the Bible tells us that she was troubled at his saying, and who wouldn't be? While she was trying to figure out what the salutation meant, Gabriel told her: "Fear not, for you have found favour with God." If you are dealing with something that is difficult to understand, something that is causing you to fear, remember, you have the power of the Highest living inside of you and you are blessed and highly favoured. Let favour triumph over fear. Favour will lead to conception because favour always makes you fruitful. This would be no ordinary conception, so Gabriel told her who was going to be conceived in her womb. "And, behold, thou shalt conceive in thy womb, and bring forth a son, and shalt call his name JESUS. He shall be great, and shall be called the Son of the Highest: and the Lord God shall give unto him the throne of his father David: And he shall reign over the house of Jacob for ever; and of his kingdom there shall be no end. Then said Mary unto the angel, How shall this be, seeing I know not a man" (Luke 1: 31-35)?

In her natural mind, Mary could not understand how it was going to take place as she was an unmarried virgin. When God is doing something supernatural in your life, don't try to figure it out with human reasoning and intellect because the supernatural can only be discerned through the Spirit. Gabriel did not leave her wondering and pondering, but gave her clarity before departing. He told her the Holy Ghost would come upon her and the power of the Highest would overshadow her. When someone receives the baptism of the Holy Ghost, the individual is impregnated with divine purpose through the overshadowing of the power of the Highest. The Greek word for overshadow as it is used there is, episkiazo, (pronounced ep-ee-skee-ad'-zo). It means, to cast a shade upon; to envelope in a haze of brilliancy; or to invest with preternatural influence. It is impossible for you to be overshadowed by the power of the Highest and your life not be radically transformed. Whatever you lacked prior to the overshadowing, you will have in abundance when He overshadows you. He equips you with everything you need to fulfill His mandate for your life; you don't have to try to make it happen.

If God says you are going to have a child and you are barren, don't get a surrogate to give birth on your behalf because you may end up with an Ishmael. Wait on the Lord, because His word will never return unto Him void.

Mary was poor, she was young, and she came from a city with a bad reputation, but she was chosen by God to birth greatness. My reader, you may have a lot of negative baggage in your life, a lot of strikes against you, or maybe you were born into poverty. Perhaps you are not college educated, or your job is menial, if you have one. People may have labeled you the least likely to succeed, but when you are chosen by God, He will overshadow you with Holy Ghost power and birth greatness out of you. He will take you places you never imagined, and use you to do things you never dreamed you could do. He would not invest the power of the Holy Ghost in you for you to live a mediocre life.

Mary was able to get it settled in her mind once Gabriel told her, for with God nothing shall be impossible. Great Women see possibility in situations that seem impossible. In life, you will face hurdles that seem insurmountable, set goals people say are unattainable, encounter mountains that seem unclimbable, but you must remember the words spoken by Gabriel to Mary: For with God nothing shall be impossible. He specializes in things that seem impossible, and your Holy Ghost power will move any mountain. Mary's speech changed once she understood; what seemed impossible at first was going to be made possible by the power of the Highest. "And Mary said, Behold the handmaid of the Lord; be it unto me according to thy word. And the angel departed from her" (Luke 1:38). I love those final words Mary spoke to the angel. Truly, they are the words of a Great Woman. They are words I use when I am expecting God to show up in challenging situations. Whatever situation you are dealing with now, take a moment and say, Lord, be it unto me according to thy word!

THE DISTINCT QUALITIES OF GREATNESS

- Divine Favor
- Chastity and Purity
- Willing to Yield to Divine Assignment
- A Joyful Sound
- Caused Another's Baby to Leap
- Facilitated the Filling of Holy Spirit
- Worshipper
- Able to Assist Another While Dealing With Her Transformation
- Conceived, Birthed and Nurtured Greatness

Chapter 15

Certain Women

A Woman's Work is Never Done; Many Hands Make Work Light

CERTAIN WOMEN—DON'T NEED THE SPOTLIGHT

God is glorified not by calling strong women but by giving His strength to weak women. —Lydia Brownback

Many of the Great Women in the Bible are unnamed, but in Luke chapter 8 the names of several women who ministered to Jesus are given. What an honor and a privilege it must have been to actually minister to Jesus when He lived on earth. Although He is no longer physically on earth, ministering to, and for Him, is at the core of every Great Woman's being. It is more precious than silver and gold. While some ministers are motivated by money, fame or the accolades they receive, Great Women minister to Jesus from a pure heart of love and dedication. I am truly inspired by the Great Women whose stories are told in this chapter.

THE TWELVE WERE WITH HIM—THE GREAT WOMEN MINISTERED TO HIM

After the encounter with the woman with the alabaster box and the negative attitudes of Simon and the other males who attended the dinner party, Luke starts chapter 8 by telling his readers: "And it came to pass afterward, that he went throughout every city and village, preaching and shewing the glad tidings of the Kingdom of God: and the twelve were with him" (Luke 8:1). The twelve were all males, handpicked by Jesus to be apostles in training for the advancement of the Kingdom. Some of them had issues that Jesus had to confront in order to prepare them to continue preaching the Gospel, and advancing the Kingdom after He ascended to heaven. One would be used by the devil to betray Jesus; one cut off a man's ear, cursed out some people at a bonfire, and denied Jesus three times. One was a doubter who had to see the nail prints in His hands to believe He had risen from the grave. When the mother of two wanted Jesus to give her sons preferred seating in His Kingdom, the other ten were filled with indignation.

There was a time when He sent out seventy to preach the Kingdom and more than likely, the twelve were among them. They came back with joy and told Jesus "... even the devils are subject to us in Your name" (Luke 10:17). Jesus did not want them boasting about what they accomplished in His name, so He corrected them: "And he said unto them, I beheld Satan as lightning fall from heaven.

Behold, I give unto you power to tread on serpents and scorpions, and over all the power of the enemy: and nothing shall by any means hurt you. Notwithstanding, in this, rejoice not that the spirits are subject unto you; but rather rejoice, because your names are written in heaven" (Luke 10:18-20).

I outlined some of the issues of the twelve in order to demonstrate the sharp contrast between them and the women Luke referred to as, 'Certain Women'. The contrast is clearly seen at the end of chapter 7 and the beginning of chapter 8. As previously stated, we saw the woman with the alabaster box castigated by Simon, the dinner host, and by the disciples who referred to her service to Jesus as 'a waste.' Jesus had to deal with a deluge of constant attacks from religious leaders, as well as the issues of the twelve. It is refreshing, therefore, to read what Luke wrote about those Certain Women at the start of chapter 8. They were Certain Women who had been healed of evil spirits, and infirmities and seemingly applied the principle found in this scripture to their daily living: "Wherefore I say unto thee, Her sins, which are many, are forgiven; for she loved much: but to whom little is forgiven, the same loveth little" (Luke 7:47).

Luke gives three of the names of these Certain Women—Mary, called Magdalene, out of whom went seven devils; Joanna, the wife of Chuza, Herod's steward; Susanna, and many others. Notice the fact there were many others, not just a few. They were focused, disciplined, dedicated and committed to the great work of Jesus. Unlike the men who were with Him jockeying for the best position, the women were not with Him for prestige or position. Luke stated that Mary Magdalene, Joanna, Susanna, and many others, ministered unto Him of their substance. They were not upfront like the twelve or boasting like the seventy. It wasn't enough for them to simply be with Him; they took of their substance and ministered to Him. Great Women are women of substance who love to be with Jesus—they show that love by ministering to Him through their inner substance, and out of their natural substance. There are Great Women all over the world who have names that are not famous, but they serve Jesus with their substance. The word ministered as it is used by Luke is derived from the Greek word diakoneo, which means to be an attendant; to wait upon (menially or as a host, friend); to serve. It comes from the root word diakonos which means, a waiter (at table or in other menial duties). Those Great Women were humble and very giving; they had no desire to be recognized. They didn't need the spotlight; they were not ministering to Jesus for a place at His right or left Hand in the Kingdom

—they were satisfied with service without a parade, pageantry, or panoply.

Some people love being with Jesus for the limelight, the recognition and the renown. Some get offended if you don't use their titles when addressing them. Job addressed this very issue—. "Let me not, I pray you, accept any man's person, neither let me give flattering titles unto man. For I know not to give flattering titles; in so doing my maker would soon take me away" (Job 32:21-22). Mary, Joanna, Susanna and the many others were great because they needed no titles; they kept Jesus and His ministry at the center of their activities. When serving required them to perform menial tasks, they were willing, and did it with joy. Great Women understand, what they do in secret, God rewards openly. I don't believe any church can survive without the service of women in general, and Great Women in particular; they bring things to the table, men are not able to. I am a firm believer in the ministry of Great Women whether it is in a leadership capacity or serving in the background. They not only bring a steely determination to get things done, they bring the soft nurturing side that fosters growth.

GREAT WOMEN ARE NOT USURPERS OF AUTHORITY

I understand the word of God instructs a woman not to usurp the authority of a man, but I believe the scripture in 1Timothy 2:12 is grossly misunderstood by some. Paul wrote: "But I suffer not a woman to teach, nor to usurp authority over the man, but to be in silence." Is Paul saying that women should be in silence in the church? Of course not, that idea is ludicrous and absurd. Scripture must be taken, line upon line, precept upon precept, here a little, there a little. If you examine the verses following, you will see Paul is speaking in the context of Eve's mishandling of the word, which caused her to be deceived. The world is a dark place when the creativity, ingenuity, and wisdom of women are stifled. If 1Timothy 2:12 is interpreted as a woman not being able to teach, but be in silence, then women would be disobeying the word of God every time they opened their mouths in church. I don't believe that was Paul's assertion; he is the same person who told the Galatians: "There is neither Jew nor Greek, there is neither bond nor free, there is neither male nor female: for ye are all one in Christ Jesus" (Galatians 3:28). I truly believe the context the scripture has to be taken in is this: a woman should not supplant the position of a male church leader without proper authority. The dictionary defines the word usurp thus: "to size and hold the power or rights of another by force or without legal authority;

to take over or occupy without right; to take the place of another without legal authority; to seize another's place, authority, or possession wrongfully" (http://www.thefreedictionary.com/usurp.) The emphasis has to be placed on the meaning of the word usurp. God's order has to be maintained for growth and development to take place. Women can open their mouths to teach, preach, and prophesy in the context of unity and the lack of any usurpation of authority. Some denominations have used Paul's words to shut down the ministry of women, robbing the Church of the greatness in those women.

Jesus, the last Adam, came and rectified that situation by giving men and women the gift of the Holy Ghost, so we can operate in wisdom, knowledge and understanding, and have power over the works of the devil. The Greek word for usurp is authenteo and it means, to act of oneself, to dominate, to exercise authority over. The usurping of authority is not limited to women; on the contrary, both men and women usurp authority when they have selfish, self-centered, and self-serving motives. The usurping of authority is wrong, whether it is done by a man or a woman, but we should not assume that Paul was making a blanket statement that every woman present and future should not teach, but must be in silence. Do you know the great things that have been accomplished and will be accomplished through the teaching grace that is upon many women?

EPIC WOMEN OF DESTINY

A day after proof-reading this chapter, my Kingdom colleague, Dr. La'Tonia sent me a Face Book post written by Axel Sippach. He is the Executive Director of the IMPACT Network, a global Apostolic network of churches and ministers, which was founded by John Eckhardt. The post blessed me tremendously; it succinctly affirmed, and encapsulated the revelation given to me by the Holy Ghost for this book. In dealing with the issue of Paul's instructions concerning women being silent in the church, I asked the Lord to give me something tangible and substantive for my readers. When I read Axel Sippach's post, I knew I had received what I needed. It included the very scripture given to me by the Holy Ghost for this book.

"SCRIPTURE DECLARES A GREAT ARMY OF WOMEN PREACHERS CAUSE THE ENEMY TO FLEE;" Psalm 68:11-12a Amplified Bible (AMP)

"The Lord gives the word (of power); the women who bear and publish (the news) are a great host. The kings of the enemies' armies, they flee, they flee! ...." OK—I'm just waiting for the "heresy hunters" to offer a rebuttal and say: "Women can't preach." It's too late for you misogynists. This is 2017. Women can do more that fry chicken in the church. The word of God is full of strong, anointed women doing great exploits for God. In Psalms 68, Scripture tells us that a great army of women preaching the Word, cause the enemies to flee. Women are God's secret weapon. They advance the Kingdom. They are bold, and they are warriors—even if they're wearing six-inch heel stilettos with their fatigues.

Women are anointed to lead, preach, prophesy, teach, cast out demons, heal the sick, evangelize, disciple, lead in worship, sing the song of the Lord, and so much more. They are anointed for breakthrough!! Women have been such a blessing to so many nations; they are incredible. They know how to move in the Spirit. They know how to open the heavens. They know how to cause demonic princes to back up in a territory, and see the enemy flee. God has had some amazing, anointed female apostolic and prophetic leaders and preachers in the church and He is about to spotlight and headline more in this season. It's not that these women necessarily want to be famous, but they want the name of Jesus to be glorified and made famous in the earth, in all the nations. They are not afraid to use whatever recognition they receive to make Him known in the earth and they realize that in Christ they have an inheritance. That inheritance includes the nations.

In the EPIC Global Network, I'm proud of the fact that we have some very powerful, anointed, apostolic, and prophetic women of God that are leaders in this tribe, who are bringing change and transformation. They are a force to be reckoned with, in advancing God's Kingdom, and glorifying the name of Jesus. They are EPIC Women of Destiny!!

For the New Testament Church, gender should not be the criteria used to determine what someone can and cannot do; Kingdom activity in the Church of Jesus Christ should be based on submission to His Lordship through the leading of the Holy Ghost. The scripture has to be taken in totality—it is dangerous to take a verse and be very dogmatic about it. It is imperative that we understand the context and culture in which it was written and based. When it comes to women in leadership, let us look at the Great Woman, Deborah, who was a prophetess and a judge.

Let us look at the Shunammite woman who told her husband, “Behold now I perceive.” Let us look at Prophetess Huldah, who spoke to the emissaries of King Josiah and said, "Thus saith the LORD God of Israel, Tell the man that sent you to me.” They were Great Women who were meek, but bold; Great Women who had strong leadership ability; Great Women who used their substance and their God-given ability to minister and serve in order to advance God’s Kingdom.

MINISTRY AND SUBSTANCE

Great Women who minister to Jesus with their substance are blessed women. They are blessed by God because He can trust them to use their substance unselfishly for His glory. There are women in physical and mental prisons, women in shelters, women on drugs, women who are battling low self-esteem, and they all have the potential to be Great Women of God. Ministry and the substance to do ministry awaits them. These women need mentors to pour into them and help them to get delivered. The power of the Holy Ghost in the mentors will help the mentees to come out of Lo-debar and be the Great Women God has called them to be. Great Women like Mary Magdalene, who was delivered of seven devils so that she could minister to Jesus with her substance; women like Joanna and Susanna who were healed of their infirmities. Televangelist, Bishop TD Jakes said, “Woman Thou Art Loosed.” I say: “Great Women you are healed; healed to minister to, and for Jesus with your substance.”

The Greek word for substance is huparchonta and it means, things extant or in hand; property or possessions; goods. The word extant means currently or actually existing not destroyed or lost. Moses, the reluctant leader, had to be asked by God, “What is that in thine hand” (Exodus 4:2)? When he told God it was a rod, God instructed him to cast it down. Once he cast down his rod, God performed miracles. The Great Women in Luke chapter 8 were willing to cast their substance down, so it could be used for the ministry of Jesus, the ministry of reconciliation. Reader, like the Great Women in the Bible, cast down your substance; tell your story!

DISTINCT QUALITIES OF GREATNESS

- Willingness to Serve
- Not Serving for Recognition
- Dedicating Substance for the King and His Kingdom
- Receiving Deliverance, Then Stepping into Ministry
- Focused
- Taking Initiative
- Team Players
- Balanced Home Life and Ministry
- Kind Hearted

Section Six

TRUE WORSHIP

Chapter 16

Martha–Mary

A Watched Pot Never Boils

MARTHA AND MARY—CHOICE AND CONSEQUENCE

f you are always trying to be normal—you will never know how amazing you can be. —Maya Angelou

There are some well-known siblings in the Bible like Moses, Aaron, and their sister, Miriam. Like all siblings there is conflict in their lives and sometimes sibling rivalry. There was a time when Miriam and Aaron spoke against Moses because he married an Ethiopian woman. I guess Miriam felt she had the right to do that because she was the eldest among the siblings. She should have understood that when God anoints and appoints someone, He will not allow family members or other people to pull rank on them because of age, finances, education or anything else. "And they said, Hath the LORD indeed spoken only by Moses? Hath he not spoken also by us? And the LORD heard it" (Numbers 12:2). You don't have to worry about people who speak against you; God hears them and He will deal with them.

Moses was the meekest man on the face of the earth. When you walk in meekness, God will deal with those who take it for weakness. God did not send an angel to deal with Miriam and Aaron; the LORD spoke suddenly to the three siblings and called them into a meeting at the tabernacle of the congregation. Miriam was a prophetess so God said: "If there be a prophet among you, I the LORD will make myself known unto him in a vision, and will speak unto him in a dream. My servant Moses is not so, who is faithful in all mine house. With him I will speak mouth to mouth" (Numbers 12:6-8). He asked Miriam and Aaron why they were not afraid to speak against His servant Moses. His anger was kindled against them and He departed. Then God left the meeting, Aaron looked at Miriam and she was leprous, white as snow. Aaron was so alarmed by what he saw that he called Moses: 'Lord' and asked his brother not to lay the sin upon them because they had been foolish. Moses cried unto the LORD asking Him to heal Miriam, but God told him the leprosy would last for seven days. There are some people you are praying for and the Lord will reverse their situation in his own time. He is teaching them an important lesson.

When Jesus was on the earth, His closest friends were siblings: Lazarus, Martha and Mary. On one occasion, he entered the village where Martha lived and she received him into her house. Luke tells us that Martha's sister, Mary, sat at the feet of Jesus and heard His word.

A lot of people are trying to get in His face, but the best place to position yourself to hear His word, is at His feet. The feet of Jesus is a place of humility. He always releases a word to those positioned at His feet, just like He did to Moses in His pre-incarnated state. Mary made a decision to prioritize the position and placed herself at the feet of Jesus. She understood the fact that the most important place to be was at His feet, listening intently to the word which proceeded out of His mouth.

CUMBERED

Unfortunately, Martha had another posture on the day she received Jesus into her house. Luke 10:40 says: Martha was cumbered with preparing and serving. We understand that when Jesus comes to the house it must be ready to receive Him. However, when He is in the house, all extra-curricular activities must cease, and everyone in the house should be at His feet. The word cumbered doesn't mean Martha was just busy serving. The Greek word for cumbered is perispao—It means to drag all around—to distract (with care). Martha was dragging around some troubles like a ball and chain, and it distracted her at a key kairos moment when Jesus entered her house. A kairos moment is a seasonable or opportune moment. When a kairos moment happens, you must not allow yourself to be distracted; you must seize the moment like Mary.

There was a spirit of distraction on Martha. She was missing a key moment and opportunity to receive a rhema word from the mouth of Jesus. Rhema is a term used to describe utterances from Jesus. Both logos and rhema describe the word but they are distinct in meaning. Logos refers to the inspired word of God and to Jesus who is the living Word. Rhema refers to the spoken word and literally means an utterance. Jesus the Logos clothed in human flesh entered the house of Martha to release the rhema, the utterance, but Martha was scurrying around the house distracted with the cares and the vicissitudes of life.

MISERY LOVES COMPANY

There is a saying I've heard since I was young "misery loves company." People who are troubled and miserable love to make other people's lives miserable. When Martha took the time to speak to Jesus, it was to ask Him if He didn't care that Mary had left her to serve alone. Martha didn't realize that she couldn't play on Jesus' emotions. Jesus is the most caring and compassionate person you will ever meet. She asked Jesus to bid Mary to come and help her.

MARTHA MARTHA!

When Jesus responds to Martha, He called her name twice. Whenever Jesus calls a person's name once it is important—when He calls twice they better make sure they drop everything and hear what the Lord is saying. Jesus said, Martha, Martha, thou art careful and troubled about many things. Martha was using the serving to mask the real issues she was dealing with; issues Jesus would deliver her from if she was willing to humble herself, emulate her sister Mary, and sit at His feet. Luke used the term cumbered about much serving but Jesus got to the root of the problem. Jesus revealed the fact that Martha was meticulous and careful about the serving but below the veneer and facade of serving—she was troubled about many things. There were some things tormenting Martha, and she attempted to have Jesus send Mary away from her posture at His feet at the wrong time.

ONE THING IS NEEDFUL—CHOOSE IT!

There is a principle in the scriptures called, "One Thing." It speaks of your ability to identify and prioritize that which is most important at any given time. A certain ruler came to Jesus and asked Him what he should do to inherit eternal life? The first set of instructions Jesus gave him was to observe the commandments. The ruler told Jesus he had kept them from his youth. He struggled with the next set of instructions given to him by Jesus. Jesus said to him, "Yet lackest thou one thing: sell all that thou hast, and distribute unto the poor, and thou shalt have treasure in heaven: and come, follow me" (Luke 18:22). When the ruler heard the instructions, he was very sorrowful: for he was very rich. Jesus saw how sorrowful he became and revealed that riches is one of the things that can hinder and distract some from entering into the Kingdom of God! In Philippians 3:13 the apostle Paul wrote: "Brethren, I count not myself to have apprehended: but this one thing I do, forgetting those things which are behind, and reaching forth unto those things which are before, I press toward the mark for the prize of the high calling of God in Christ Jesus."

THE PRIZE OF THE HIGH CALLING

The prize of the high calling is to carry and manifest the Glory of God. This prestigious place cannot be attained without self-denial, the death of the flesh, forsaking all to follow Jesus and to sit at His feet. Mary was willing to do that, but Martha was not. Jesus told Martha, "but one thing is needful" (Luke 10:42). There is no mystery to the needful thing. The needful thing is for you to forsake everything to posture yourself at the feet of Jesus. Every distraction must be dealt with, and every hindrance must be moved out of the way. Zacchaeus, a rich publican, sought to see Jesus. There were certain Greeks who came to worship at the feast who went to Philip and appealed to him saying: "Sir, we would see Jesus." It is not enough to see Him, but you must desire to sit at His feet like Mary. You must desire like Paul to know Him in the power of His resurrection and the fellowship of His suffering. At His feet, we will receive divine revelation and prophetic instructions.

IT'S YOUR CHOICE

Jesus told Martha that Mary chose the good part, and that which she chose shall not be taken away from her. All of us have the same number of hours in a day, but each of us must choose what and where we will allocate our precious time. Sitting at the feet of Jesus is so important. It has to be like the pearl of great price, and the treasure that was hid in the field. When you find it, you must part with everything to obtain it. There is a saying in Spanish: tiempo es oro—time is gold; time is money. Great Women, like Mary, refuse to be distracted by the superficial and the superfluous. They know how to prioritize the important things, like putting the Kingdom first. The King of Kings, the Lord of Lords, the Conquering Lion of the Tribe of Judah, came to the house of Martha, and she missed her kairos time and moment of visitation; PLEASE DON'T MISS YOURS!

Distinct Qualities of Greatness

- Knows When to Serve and When to Be Still
- Makes the Right Choices
- Knows How to Submit to Leadership
- Knows When to Seize the Moment
- Knows How to Prioritize
- Not Distracted by the Activities of Others
- Does Not Allow Anyone or Anything to Pull Her Away From the Feet of Jesus
- Meek and Humble
- Jesus Lover

The Woman With The Alabaster Box

One Man's Trash is Another Man's Treasure

THE WOMAN WITH THE ALABASTER BOX

*Y**ou're a Diamond Dear—they can't break you. —Source Unknown*

The Lord is not looking for perfect people—He is looking for people to perfect. He chooses and uses flawed individuals to manifest His Divine Will. CC Winans has a beautiful song called 'Alabaster Box.' The Great Woman in this chapter came to worship Jesus with an alabaster box. She did not have the fame or fortune of Sister CC. As a matter of fact, she had a negative reputation in her community. To her credit, she did not allow what people thought about her to stop her from pouring the oil upon the Master from her box of alabaster.

Her story is found in Matthew 26:7, Mark 14:3, and Luke 7:37. Luke tells the reader that a Pharisee desired Jesus to eat with him. Jesus was always gracious when He was invited to a home to eat, so he acquiesced. There are times when He invites Himself, as He did with Zacchaeus. There are times when He stands at the door and knocks, waiting for someone to let Him in, so he could sup with them. The Pharisee took the initiative to invite Jesus, but he didn't know what would transpire at the dinner party. While Jesus is there, an unnamed woman in the city, a woman who is listed as a sinner, when she knew that Jesus was dining in the house, came in with an alabaster box.

THE PHARISEE—SO SAD, YOU SEE

To understand her boldness, I have to tell you who the Pharisees were. According to the Blue Letter Bible, "The word Pharisee is derived from an Aramaic word meaning, 'separated'. They were a group that held to the immortality of the soul, the resurrection of the dead, and punishment in future life. In Jesus' day, the Pharisees practiced righteousness externally. They were more concerned with the outward appearance than inward feeling. They were the worst persecutors of Jesus and the objects of His strongest criticism. They loathed and looked down upon sinners; that meant, for the woman with the alabaster box to go to a Pharisee's house, she had to be bold. She refused to be denied. She knew the scorn she would receive for daring to go into a Pharisee's house, but she had done her homework, like the woman of Tyre and Sidon who crashed a house gathering where Jesus was spending some quiet time. The Bible states, "... he arose and went into the borders of Tyre and Sidon, and entered into an house, and would have no man know it: but he could not be hid" (Mark 7:24).

GIVE ME MY CRUMMY MIRACLE

Both women did their reconnaissance and found where Jesus was going to be and both made a bold faith move. Great Women are women of faith who will find Jesus wherever He is. The woman of Tyre and Sidon was a Syrophoenician Greek by nationality. She had a daughter with a devil and she was desperate to get to Jesus. Don't ever try to get in the way of a mother with a sick child because she will run you over. She came into the house, and fell at Jesus' feet because Great Women stay at the feet of Jesus. She asked Jesus to cast the devil out of her daughter. "But Jesus said unto her, let the children first be filled: for it is not meet to take the children's bread, and to cast it unto the dogs" (Luke 7:27). She secured the healing for her daughter because she did not get offended with Jesus. She said, "Yes, Lord: yet the dogs under the table eat of the children's crumbs" (Verse 28). In other words—I am whatever you say I am, but give me my crummy miracle.

So, the woman who is called a sinner is in the Pharisee's house with Jesus and the disciples. She does not enter the house empty handed, but brings her alabaster box. Matthew and Mark said: she had an alabaster box of ointment of spikenard, very precious. According to Barnes' Notes on the Bible, "The 'alabaster' is a species of marble, distinguished for being light, and of a beautiful white color, almost transparent." Barnes goes on to say, "It was an ointment of great value that was rare and difficult to be obtained." She had a reputation in her neighborhood, but she brought something of great value to Jesus. She stood behind Jesus, at His feet, which speaks of her humility. She wept and washed His feet with her tears, and wiped them with her hair. She kissed His feet, and anointed them with the oil from her alabaster box. What an awesome woman. What guts it must have taken to know what people thought about her, but to ignore them and bring her worship to Jesus in a posture of great humility.

Contrast Jesus' dinner host, the Pharisee, to that great woman. When he saw what the woman did he spoke within himself, criticizing Jesus. He had the audacity criticizing Jesus, since Matthew identifies him as Simon, the leper. I guess he didn't realize that Jesus could discern the thoughts of his vain, religious mind. He said: "This man, if he were a prophet, would have known who and what manner of woman this is that toucheth Him: for she is a sinner" (Luke 7:39). He classed Jesus as, "this man", questioned the prophetic mantle He carried, and called the woman a sinner.

When you decide to press beyond the borders of religion to worship Jesus, expect religion to come against you and call you anything but a child of God. Great Women do not deny the fact they have issues—they just refuse to allow anyone to stop them from pouring on the Master, the oil of worship from their box of alabaster.

Jesus did not give the Pharisee a pass. He probably thought he got away with his insult because he spoke it within himself, but you cannot hide anything from Jesus—He is 'All Knowing', He is Omniscient. He is the Word, and the Bible states, "For the word of God is quick, and powerful, and sharper than any two-edged sword, piercing even to the dividing asunder of soul and spirit, and of the joints and marrow, and is a discerner of the thoughts and intents of the heart" (Hebrews 4:12). And Jesus answering said unto him, Simon, I have somewhat to say unto thee. And he saith, Master, say on. "Now he is calling Jesus Master because Jesus peeped his card. As He often does when He is in teaching mode, Jesus spoke to him in a story. "There was a certain creditor which had two debtors: the one owed five hundred pence, and the other fifty. And when they had nothing to pay, he frankly forgave them both. Tell me therefore, which of them will love him most? Simon answered and said, I suppose that he, to whom he forgave most. And he said unto him, Thou hast rightly judged" (Luke 7:40-43).

Then Jesus turned to the woman and told Simon: "Seest thou this woman? I entered into thine house, thou gravest me no water for my feet: but she hath washed my feet with tears, and wiped them with the hairs of her head. Thou gavest me no kiss: but this woman since the time I came in hath not ceased to kiss my feet. My head with oil thou didst not anoint: but this woman hath anointed my feet with ointment. Wherefore I say unto thee, Her sins, which are many, are forgiven; for she loved much: but to whom little is forgiven, the same loveth little. And He said unto her, Thy sins are forgiven" (Luke 7:44-48). All I can say is WOW! What an encounter. She came in with the label 'sinner' attached to her and left with total forgiveness, while the religious leader received an open rebuke because of his accusations and lack of compassion. Jesus' last words to the Great Woman were, "Thy sins are forgiven." The other guests who sat at meat with Him were so astonished they asked within themselves, "Who is this that forgiveth sins also?" My answer to everyone, especially those of a different belief is: He is THEANTHROPOS—The GOD—MAN.

According to Mark's gospel, the Pharisee was not the only person at the dinner who was indignant when the woman broke her alabaster box and anointed Jesus. Mark wrote, "There were some that had indignation within themselves, and said, Why was this waste of the ointment made" (Mark 14:4)? Can you imagine someone thinking that anointing Jesus with a precious ointment was a waste? Mark wrote, "For it might have been sold for more than three hundred pence, and have been given to the poor. And they murmured against her" (Mark 14:5). They were chauvinistic and misogynistic; attacking the precious woman because she worshipped Jesus with meekness and brokenness. They should have followed her lead. Jesus rebuked them and said, "Let her alone; why trouble ye her? She hath wrought a good work on me. For ye have the poor with you always, and whensoever ye will ye may do them good: but me ye have not always. She hath done what she could: she is come aforehand to anoint my body to the burying. Verily I say unto you, wheresoever this gospel shall be preached throughout the whole world, this also that she hath done shall be spoken of for a memorial of her" (Mark 14:6-9). HALLELUJAH!!! That is why she is a Great Woman. She was bold, she took initiative, and she was not intimidated by male vain, religious chauvinism.

DISTINCT QUALITIES OF GREATNESS

- Fearless not Fearful
- Risk Taker
- Takes Initiative
- Must See Jesus
- Worshipper
- Does Not Allow People's Negativity to Keep Her From Connecting to Jesus
- Great Humility
- Refuse to Be Denied
- Giver, Not a Taker

The Woman at the Well

"Freedom Cannot Be Attained Unless Women Have Been Emancipated from All Forms of Oppression" Nelson Mandela

THE WOMAN AT THE WELL —PURSUE Him NOT him

o woman wants to be in submission to a man who isn't in submission to God. —T.D. Jakes

The Biblical story of the Woman at the Well is one that blesses me every time I read it. She is in my Hall of Faith of Great Women because her encounter with Jesus radically transformed her life. It motivated her to go back to her village and share the good news of that encounter with Jesus, which I believe radically transformed the village.

At a certain point in time Jesus left Judaea, departed again into Galilee, then decided it was necessary to go through Samaria. During that time opposition was rising against Jesus, especially from the Pharisees. They were against Jesus' popularity and His message because it challenged many of their teachings. Jesus was just starting His ministry; it was not time for Him to confront the Pharisees and other religious leaders, so He left Jerusalem and travelled north toward Galilee. The trip through Samaria was not a route Jews would take when traveling; the Jews loathed the Samaritans because they were a mixed race who set up an alternative center of worship on Mount Gerazim.

THE SAMARITANS

According to the commentary on John 4 in the Life Application Bible, The Samaritans came into being when the Northern Kingdom with its capital at Samaria fell to the Assyrians. Many Jews were deported to Assyria and after their deportation, foreigners were brought in to settle the land and to help keep the peace (2 Kings 17:24). The intermarriage between those foreigners and the remaining Jews led to a mixed race, impure in the opinion of Jews who lived in the Southern Kingdom. The pure Jews hated this mixed race called Samaritans because they felt they had betrayed their people and nation. Jesus was not one to be caught up in geographical and ethnic prejudices. He came to seek and to save the lost—besides, the route through Samaria was the shorter one for His trip. Jesus was not going to allow His trip to take longer than necessary because of ethnic prejudice.

NATURAL OR LIVING WATER?

On His journey, Jesus arrived at a place in Samaria called Sychar. It was near the land that Jacob gave to his son Joseph. Jacob's well was there and Jesus sat on it because He was weary from His Journey. John is careful to tell us that it was the sixth hour, which meant it was 12 noon. Six is the number of man and the weakness of the flesh. His disciples had gone into the city to buy meat. Wells were almost always located outside of the city near the main road and morning and evening, twice a day, women came to the well to draw water. They usually did not come to the well at noon because of the heat of the sun. While Jesus is at the well a woman comes to draw water and He engages her in conversation. Jesus said, "Give me to drink" (John 4:7). We are used to Jesus giving us drink, but He asked the woman to give Him water to drink. It was not only to quench His thirst; it was a strategy to lead her to eternal life. The woman was shocked that Jesus even spoke to her, much less asked her to give Him water to drink. She asked Him how it was that He, being a Jew, would ask her a Samaritan woman for a drink—since the Jews had no dealings with the Samaritans. She had no knowledge of Jesus' identity, but she was about to get the revelation. This is one of the stories in the Bible that evidences the fact that racism is un-Godly.

Jesus went right to the heart of the matter by telling her that if she knew the gift of God who asked her for a drink, she would have asked Him, and He would have given her living water. Now you see that Jesus had to go through Samaria; not because it represented a shorter route to His destination. Now you see the main reason why He sat on the well. His thirst was secondary to His desire to see the life of the Samaritan Woman and her village transformed. He did not want her to return to her village in the same condition, with the same reputation with which she left; that reputation probably was the reason why she came to the well at noon. She did not expect to see anyone there because of the heat of the noon-day sun. She was in the heat of the SUN, but she was about to be cooled off by Living Water from the SON. She came to the well for natural water, but would leave with living water. Natural water quenches physical thirst; living water quenches spiritual thirst.

Jesus maneuvered her conversation from ethnic prejudice to the difference between natural and living water. He that winneth souls is wise (Proverbs 11:30b). An unwise person would have allowed himself to get caught up in the ethnic and racial divide.

Jesus had the Spirit without measure; He had wisdom without measure. His conversations were always focused and to the point. At first she thought Jesus was referring to the natural water in the well, so she questioned Him about not having anything with which to draw the water. She soon realized He was referring to a different water. She told Him the well was deep, so where would He get the living water. She asked Him if He was greater than their Father Jacob, who was a patriarch to the Samaritans. She told Jesus that Jacob gave them the well, drank from it himself, and so did his children and cattle. She knew her history, but she was oblivious to the true identity of the person speaking with her—even when He gave her the clue that He could give her living water.

It was just one clue, so she would need deeper teaching. Jesus went deeper when He told her: "Whosoever drinketh of this water shall thirst again: But Whosoever drinketh of the water that I shall give him shall never thirst: but the water that I shall give him shall be in him a well of water springing up into everlasting life" (John 4:14). To her credit, the Samaritan woman asked Jesus to give her that water so she would not thirst again, neither have to draw from the well. I do not know if she was thinking about her physical thirst when Jesus spoke about spiritual thirst and eternal life. I do know, she wanted to make sure she did not have to come back to the well to draw water, especially in the heat of the noon day. At that juncture Jesus switched the conversation and told her, "Go, call thy husband, and come hither." Jesus was, and is the Master Strategist. Here you see Him tactically leading the precious woman at the well to eternal life; methodically breaking down barriers of ethnic separation; teaching her the difference between natural and spiritual, between vain religion and true worship.

THE SEVENTH MAN—THE GOD MAN!

The woman thought she could side-step the issue of her home life by telling Jesus she had no husband, but Jesus was about to deal with that important issue. He told her she spoke right when she said she had no husband because she had five husbands, and her current lover was not her husband. The number five meant she was looking for grace, but she could not find it in her five husbands, so she got in the flesh and hooked up with a sixth man. When Jesus encountered her at the well she met the seventh man—He is the perfect man, the only man who could give her the living water that sprang up into eternal life.

The woman at the well had five husbands plus a man she was not married to; when she met Jesus, she met God clothed in humanity. When Jesus went deep into her life, she realized He was not just any Jew speaking to her. She told Jesus, "Sir, I perceive that thou art a prophet." She knew He had to be a prophet to know such personal things about her home life without knowing her. He was so much more than a prophet. He was the true Master Prophet and then some.

TRUE WORSHIPPERS

When the woman realized that Jesus was flowing prophetically, she made an attempt to shift the conversation to worship. She told Jesus that her fathers worshipped in that mountain, and the Jews were saying Jerusalem was the place where men ought to worship. She was referring to Mount Gerazim, but no mountain, no matter how tall, could be compared to the great city of Jerusalem. Jesus was about to give her some deep teaching on true worship. Jesus saith unto her, "Woman, believe me, the hour cometh, when ye shall neither in this mountain, nor yet at Jerusalem, worshipped the Father." Jesus informed her of a coming paradigm shift in the manner in which God would be worshiped. I believe she is the first person who received that revelation from Jesus. What a privilege!

TRUE WORSHIP

Jesus told her she did not know worship, because salvation was of the Jews. Her lack of understanding of true worship was evidenced by the fact that she thought because her fathers worshiped at Mount Gerazim, they were true worshipers. Jerusalem was the center of worship at that time. Jesus was teaching her that the hour was coming when worship would not be based on a physical or geographical location. He told her, "But the hour cometh, and now is, when the true worshippers shall worship the Father in spirit and in truth: for the Father seeketh such to worship. God is a Spirit: and they that worship him must worship him in spirit and in truth" (John 4: 23-24). True worship cannot be confined to a certain location because True worship is Spirit-led worship, and the Spirit is not limited or confined to a certain place.

The teaching on True Worship became so heavy, the woman told Jesus that Messias, who was called Christ, was coming and when He came He would tell them all things. Her understanding was becoming clearer because of the time Jesus spent giving her Kingdom revelation. She was in the right lane when she talked about the coming of Messias, but she had not arrived at the destination Jesus was leading her to because she did not know that He was Messias. "Jesus saith unto her, I that speak unto thee am He" (John 4: 26).

Woman at the Well
LEAVE YOUR WATER POT

It took a while to get to the place where her greatness manifested; when she first encountered Jesus she lacked knowledge of true spirituality. Once she came into the fullness, her greatness began to shine as bright as the noon-day Sun which shone overhead when she came with her water-pot to draw from the well. Once Jesus revealed His true identity her priorities shifted from natural to spiritual, from earthly to Kingdom. She left her water-pot, went into the city and told the men: "Come, see a man, which told me all things that ever I did: Is not this the Christ" (John 4:29)?

Reader—what is the water-pot that you have to leave behind in-order to tell people about Jesus the Messiah? Leaving your water-pot means making the sacrifices necessary to see people's lives transformed by the knowledge of Jesus. Leaving your water-pot means putting the Kingdom before your personal needs and knowing when you do that, all things will be added unto you. Great Women, like the woman at the well, make a radical move when Messiah reveals Himself to them. Revelation will make you radical. Remember, she had a negative reputation when she came to the well because of some lifestyle choices, but Jesus dealt with all of them and she went back to the city totally transformed.

Men who are secure in who God has called them to be have no problem following a Great Woman. At the words of the Great Woman who came to the well, the men went out of the city, and came to Jesus. Many of the Samaritans of the city believed on Jesus because of the saying of the woman. Great Woman, some men will not listen to you no matter how great you are because they are insecure and bound by a misogynistic, chauvinistic spirit. At the request of the Samaritans, Jesus stayed two days in their city ministering to them; many more Samaritans believed Him when they heard the words from His mouth. As the facilitator, this Great Woman has to be considered the first evangelist of the New Testament!

DISTINCT QUALITIES OF GREATNESS

- Thirsty For Living Water
- Shares Her Living Water
- Willing to Learn
- Evangelize
- Left Her Water Pot to Fulfill a Greater Calling
- Learns the Meaning of True Worship
- Willing to Tell Others About the Impact Jesus Had On Her Life
- Willing to Receive Truth
- Great Before and After Picture

When The
STORM BREAKS

Abigail

"A Wise Woman Wishes to Be No One's Enemy; A Wise Woman Refuses to Be Anyone's Victim"
Maya Angelou

ABIGAIL—BRILLIANT STRATEGIST

man with dreams needs a woman with vision.

When the Amalakites burned Ziklag and took the women and children belonging to David and his men captive, one of David's wives is mentioned. Although she is married to David at the time, the writer describes her as Abigail, the wife of Nabal, the Carmelite. I believe the Holy Spirit had the writer here describe her that way to draw the reader's attention to the events that took place between David and Nabal in which Abigail was able to diffuse a toxic situation with quick thinking and wise strategy. "Part of being a Great Woman is knowing what to do, what to say, what not to do and what not to say" (M. Hardy, personal communication, December 24, 2016).

Abigail is described in 1 Samuel 25 as a woman of "good understanding," who had a "beautiful countenance." She was not only a pretty face, but also a woman of wisdom and understanding.There is a seeming paradox in her life in terms of the man she chose to marry. Her husband, Nabal, is described as churlish and evil in his doings. Dictionary.com defines churlish as—boorish, rude, mean and difficult to work with. The KJV online dictionary defines churlish as; selfish; narrow-minded; avaricious, obstinate and unfeeling. The biblical definition of the name Nabal is foolish or fool.

WISE WOMAN—DO NOT MARRY A FOOL!!!

There are many women who will read this book and readily admit that at some point in their lives they made a decision to marry a certain individual and that choice turned out to be foolish. They did their best to make the marriage work, but the Nabal they married refused to allow the greatness in the wife they had, to aid in their growth and development. The Bible does not give us any details pertaining to what Nabal was like when he courted and married the Great Woman, Abigail, but there are some clues. When you examine his life as it is described in the Bible, he was a wealthy and prosperous man. It is possible that Abigail's parents arranged the marriage for the protection and financial security he was able to provide. He is described in 1 Samuel 25:2 as being very great, not because of wisdom, love and kindness, but because of his possessions.

He received a good thing when he married Abigail, but his obstinacy, and his selfishness hindered him from receiving the favor she brought to the marriage. His inability to work with others would eventually cause his demise, and another man, David, would reap the benefits from the wife Nabal did not cherish because he was CHURLISH!

David faced extreme conditions and difficulties when he fled the mad, murderous attempts on his life by King Saul. At one point in his sojourn, David heard in the wilderness that Nabal was shearing his sheep. He sent ten young men to greet Nabal to speak a word of peace to him and to petition him for some provision. David instructed the young men to tell him how they had protected his shepherds while they were with them. They were not hurt and nothing was taken from them. David was very humble in his request as revealed in 1 Samuel 25:8 "Wherefore let the young men find favour in thine eyes; for we come in a good day: give, I pray thee, whatsoever cometh to thine hand unto thy servants, and to thy son David."

Nabal's response showed the churlishness of his nature, his lack of discernment and gives us a great contrast between his character and the character of Abigail. And Nabal answered David's servants, and said, "Who is David? And who is the son of Jessie? There be many servants now a days that break away every man from his master. Shall I then take my bread, and my water, and my flesh that I have killed for my shearers, and give it unto men, whom I know not whence they be." (1 Samuel 25; 10-11).
When the young men told David what Nabal said, he was livid and told them to, gird on their sword. David was a man after God's own heart and a prolific worshipper, but he was not someone to play with. The fact that he took four hundred men with him when he decided to visit Nabal is proof he meant business. Nabal's foolishness caused him to lose his life and to lose his wife.

DIFFUSING AN EXPLOSIVE SITUATION

There is a reason why the book of Proverbs describes wisdom with a feminine pronoun. Great Women have the ability to bring wisdom, counsel and understanding to a volatile situation.You see the manifestation of that principle in the action Abigail took when she realized what would result from her husband's foolish and disrespectful behavior in responding to David's request. One of the young men who worked for Nabal told Abigail what her husband had done and described to her how good David was to them when they were in the field. He told her, "David and his men were a wall unto us both night and day, all the while we were in the fields." He described Nabal as a son of Belial who a man could not speak to.

If Abigail was great for no other reason she was great for tolerating such a horrible man. There are many men who are so wrapped up in themselves they cannot discern who and what it is, that is around them to bless them. Nabal had great possessions and in Abigail he had a Great Woman who could have helped him to obtain favor with the king, but he refused to change his ways. Once she heard the news she did what all Great Women do, she made haste and prepared to take the type of action that would diffuse the impending explosive situation. She took two hundred loaves, two bottles of wine, and five sheep ready dressed, five measures of parched corn, a hundred clusters of raisins, and two hundred cakes of figs to bless David and his men. It is often said that the way to a man's heart is through his stomach and Abigail knew that, because she was a thinking woman, a woman of action and a woman of good understanding.

GREAT WOMAN—YOU CAN'T TELL HIM EVERYTHING

Married couples will tell you communication is a very important skill in marriage as it is a trait that is most closely linked to its success or failure. They will also tell you that it is not good to keep secrets from your spouse, but based on experience you can't tell your husband everything if he is churlish, childish, and foolish. In her great wisdom and understanding, Abigail did not tell her husband what she planned to bring to David and his men because she knew he would act like a fool. Many women have shared their plans, their visions, and their expectations with their husbands only for them to shoot them down with criticism, doubt and a lack of enthusiasm. When Abigail met David, he was wroth because he felt his kindness towards Nabal was in vain and Nabal had returned evil for his good. When Abigail saw him, she bowed herself to the ground which was customary for one meeting a king. She not only had wisdom and good understanding, but she had a great sense of discernment to identify the greatness in David even though he was in a difficult season when he encountered her and her husband, Nabal. Great Women are discerning women who are able to spot a Diamond In The Rough! They are able to see beyond the facade, beyond the veneer of roughness, to cultivate the precious gem on the inside.

FRONTLINE WARRIORS

Sandy Phanazee in her 31—Day Women's Devotional writes: "You are called to be a front-line warrior. Front-line warriors face the fierceness of the battle; it's rough, it's hard and it requires a lot, but I handpicked you from a child and knew these days of warfare would come. I also know that you will fight; and through the fight, you will be made stronger and better equipped to fight the next battle (Day 9)."

Great Women, like Abigail, are frontline warriors willing to take the hit for their husbands even when they behave like fools. Her first words to David paint a very beautiful picture of her humility, unselfishness, and character traits shared by all the Great Women in this book, and all the Great Women who read this book. She told David: "Upon me, my Lord, upon me let this iniquity be: and let thine handmaid, I pray thee, speak in thine audience, and hear the words of thine handmaiden" (1Samuel 25:24). She went on to say: "Let not my Lord, I pray thee, regard this man of Belial, even Nabal: for as his name is, so is he; Nabal is his name, and folly is with him: but I thine handmaid saw not the young men of my Lord, whom thou didst send" (1 Samuel 25:25).

She presented her case to David in a clear, articulate manner and let him know that things transpired the way they did because of the folly of her husband, and the fact that she did not see the young men he sent. She told David of the blessings she brought for him and the young men, then she spoke by the Spirit concerning what the Lord would make of David. As far as I'm concerned, she was a true prophetic intercessor because she stood in the gap, took ownership of the situation, and spoke to David's destiny in God. She didn't spend a lot of time speaking to him about Nabal. After she told him of the character of Nabal, she systematically told David of the greatness that was before him. Great Women don't spend a lot of time pointing out another individual's shortcomings; they use their mouths to speak life, to speak purpose, assignment and destiny.

LOOK AT THE BIG PICTURE

Great Women know how to help others to focus on the big picture and that is exactly what Abigail did when she met with David. Sometimes our anger can cause us to miss the big picture even though the anger is justified. David was right to be angry with Nabal for his rudeness, but Abigail wanted him to focus more on where he was going, not what Nabal had done. Please read her words to him and you will see exactly how dynamic that sister was. She told David that after the Lord had done all the good to him that He had spoken, the folly from Nabal would be of no grief to him nor offensive to his heart. She asked David to remember her when the Lord had dealt with him, and her piety and humility caused David's anger to subside to the place where he said to her, "Blessed be the LORD God of Israel, which sent thee this day to meet me." Great Women are sent women, they are Apostolic women who rise to their divine assignment no matter how difficult it is. They willingly release their time, energy and their finances to bless the King.

David told Abigail that the advice she had given him kept him from shedding blood and destroying Nabal and everything he possessed. He received the provisions she brought for him and pronounced a blessing over her by saying, "Go up in peace to thine house; see, I have hearkened to thy voice, and have accepted thy person." Great Women speak words of good counsel, wisdom and understanding that bring change and transformation. Their words soothe and calm the savage beast of vengeance that can manifest in us when we feel disrespected.

We can learn a great deal from Abigail's actions. We must use the kind of quick thinking and swift action she used to diffuse a toxic and volatile situation. We can learn true humility from her, how to give good advice and speak with wisdom. How to diffuse and not exacerbate and escalate a terrible situation. I see a common thread woven through the fabric of the life of Abigail and all Great Women; they exhibit, exemplify and exude poise in the midst of pressure.

A MOMENT OF TRANSPARENCY—I WAS A NABAL

No matter how great a man is, when he finds his wife, his good thing, she is a gift that he receives to help him become greater. Every Great Woman at some point in her life will be connected to a Nabal, whether through friendship, courtship or matrimony. If a man is to achieve greater, he has to realize that in all men there are some Nabal-like traits and attributes. The Abigail in their lives are there to help them mature to a level where those traits do not stagnate their development and eventually destroy them. In a moment of transparency—I must admit, if it had not been for the Abigail-like qualities in my wife, Paulette, I would not be in the place or posture that I am today. All glory and honor belong to God for saving, delivering and giving me not another chance, but many chances to succeed.

My wife is a key instrument used by God to facilitate that success. This book is my eleventh book. I've been interviewed on Christian Television before an audience of millions; I've ministered to great and small and seen the manifestation of the glory of God transform people's lives, but I did not get here by myself.

When my Abigail, Paulette Donaldson, warned me not to take that ill-fated trip to England, my Nabal nature came out. I obstinately ignored her advice, to my own detriment. That gave her one of many chances when she could have thrown in the towel, but instead, she was loving, she was supportive, and she kept praying and interceding on my behalf. God uses an Abigail to be a compass or a rudder to steer the life of her husband in a positive direction, but when he allows his Nabal-like character to dominate and control him, his life will end up in disaster. Nabal died of a heart attack while in a drunken stupor and reveling in a gluttonous feast.

The target audience for this book is primarily women, however, I pray that God gets it into the hands of men who need to understand the importance of cherishing the Abigails that enter their lives and not allowing churlish attitudes to derail their destiny.

DISTINCT QUALITIES OF GREATNESS

- Wisdom
- Good Understanding
- Excellent Strategist
- Woman of Action
- Kindness
- Quick Thinker
- Great Counselor
- Great Humility
- Apt to Teach

Rahab

Don't Judge a Book by Its Cover

RAHAB—FROM THE WHOREHOUSE TO THE LORD'S HOUSE

successful woman is one who can build a firm foundation with the bricks others have thrown at her. —Source Unknown

Jesus has some very interesting individuals in His genealogy and one of the most interesting is a woman by the name of Rahab. Her moniker in the Bible is Rahab, the harlot, a title no woman in her right mind would want attached to her name. She made it into my Hall of Fame of Great Women because of the actions she took in accommodating the spies sent by God to check out the Promised Land. Let's be honest, if given the opportunity to choose the individuals who would make up the lineage of Messiah, the Savior of the world, we probably would not choose a woman called Rahab, the harlot. She epitomizes the awesome, wonderful grace of God and is testimony to the fact that He will use whomsoever He chooses to fulfill His purpose and His plans. Think about it, of all the houses, of all the people in Jericho the Lord could have used to strategically position spies, he chose the house of Rahab, the harlot. The first time I heard the name and the accompanying words next to her name, I was like, WOW! To say I was intrigued would be a gross understatement. The sovereignty of God is above and beyond human understanding and reproach. The apostle Paul confirms this in Romans 11:33 when he wrote: "O the depth of the riches both of the wisdom and knowledge of God! how unsearchable are his judgments, and his ways past finding out! For who hath known the mind of the Lord? or who hath been his counsellor?"

A HOOKER WITH A HEART FOR GOD

In an online article for todayschristianwoman.com, Liz Curtis Higgs starts the article with this headline: Rahab: A Hooker with a Heart for God. She went on to write: "call her a lady of the evening, if you like, or a streetwalker. Yet the Bible calls Rahab worthy, listing her among the faithful in Hebrews 11." God doesn't choose women because they are great. He chooses them to make them great. He doesn't choose perfect people. He perfects the people He chooses. He chose and continues to choose women from all walks of life; women of different creeds and colors to manifest His Glory, to fulfill His purpose. Rahab was chosen at a critical point in the history of His chosen nation, Israel. After the death of Moses, the LORD spoke to Moses' minister Joshua to lead the people over the River

Jordan to the land He had given them. Joshua sent two men on a secret mission to spy in Jericho, the first land of conquest. The Bible does not give us the details, but somehow they wound up in the Whore House. They were not there for carnal, sensual pleasures, like Samson when he went into the house of Delilah. Someone told the king of Jericho that some of the children of Israel came to Jericho in the night to search out the country. Their cover was blown and that meant certain death for them, for Rahab, and for everyone living in her house. The king sent word to Rahab to bring forth the men.

It was a pivotal moment for Rahab—-should she risk her life by continuing to hide the spies or obey the king's edict? Great Women rise to the occasion and Rahab was one. She would rise like Abigail in the face of an imminent threat. Rahab hid the spies and sent word to the king that some men came to her, but she did not know where they were. She told the king that prior to the shutting of the gate that evening, the men went out, but he could catch them if he went after them. Rahab had actually hidden the spies on the roof of her house. I would imagine that over the years some have asked the question, "When, and if it is ok to tell a lie." My response is, Rahab was not exactly a paragon of virtue, but in lying to the king of Jericho she went for the greater good.

Rahab had the reputation of being a harlot, a hooker, a lady of the evening, and I believe, beyond a shadow of a doubt, that when the spies chose her house it ceased to be a house of ill repute, and a den of iniquity. She had heard what the LORD did when the Israelites came out of Egypt. And she said unto the men: "I know the LORD hath given you the land, and that your terror is fallen upon us, and that all the inhabitants of the land faint because of you" (Joshua 2:9). She asked the spies to show kindness unto her father's house since she had shown them kindness. She asked them to give her a true token. Her request demonstrated a common thread found in Great Women—Unselfishness. She risked her life when she hid them and now she petitioned them, not for herself, but for her father, mother, her brethren and her sisters. The men promised to deal kindly with her once the LORD gave them the land.

One of the common denominators I've witnessed in the lives of the Great Women of the Bible and the Great Women I've encountered in my lifetime is this—They are women of action, women who are not afraid to take risks, women who are initiators not imitators.

Rahab had the pedigree of greatness because she took immediate action to secure the safety of the spies. She gave them explicit instructions which helped them to successfully complete their mission. She told them to get to the mountain, and hide themselves for three days. The mountain represents a high place and the number three represents completion and resurrection. The men reciprocated by giving her explicit instructions to follow when they returned to conquer the city. They told her when they returned she should bind the line of scarlet thread they gave her in the window. The men told her to bring her father, her mother, her brethren and her sisters into her house and they would be protected.

THE TOKEN—THE SCARLET THREAD

Barnes notes on the Bible in the biblehub.com commentary has this to say about the Scarlet Thread: "The "line" or cord was spun of threads dyed with cochineal: i. e., of a deep and bright scarlet color. The color would catch the eye at once, and supplied an obvious token by which the house of Rahab might be distinguished. The use of scarlet in the Levitical rites, especially in those more closely connected with the idea of putting away of sin and its consequences, naturally led the fathers, from Clement of Rome onward, to see in this scarlet thread no less than in the blood of the Passover, an emblem of salvation by the Blood of Christ; a salvation common alike to Christ's messengers and to those whom they visit."

The men followed her instructions to the letter and dwelt in the mountain for three days, then returned and told Joshua all that happened to them. "And they said to Joshua, Truly the LORD hath delivered into our hands all the land; for even all the inhabitants of the country do faint because of us" (Joshua 2:24). Rahab's bold brave action facilitated and set in motion the chain of events that led to the victory. Isaiah 1:18 declares: Come now, and let us reason together, saith the Lord: though your sins be as scarlet, they shall be as white as snow; though they be red like crimson, they shall be as wool. Like the woman at the well who looked for comfort in the arms of men until she met the God-Man, Jesus Christ—like the woman with the Alabaster Box who was labeled a sinner—like Mary Magdalene who had seven demons cast out of her by Jesus—like you and me—Rahab had sins like scarlet, but she was able to reason with the men of God and received deliverance for her household. From the whore house to The LORD's house, what a Mighty God we serve. Some of us came from the jail house to the LORD's house; some came from the crack house, some from the heroin shooting gallery.

Whatever house of sin you find yourself in at the present time, please know this: NO SIN, no matter how deep, dark or dirty, can negate or nullify the effectiveness of the BLOOD of JESUS CHRIST.

THE LAMB'S BOOK OF LIFE—A NEW NAME

He is the Lamb of God provided to take away the sins of the world. The Bible says the Lamb was slain from the foundation of the world. Before the foundation of the world God had prepared for the deliverance of Rahab's household and your household. It would have been awesome enough for Rahab's name to be mentioned in the Bible, but she holds the precious distinction of being in the lineage of Jesus and making it into the Hall of Faith listed in Hebrews 11. Your name and my name are not in the Bible for obvious reasons, but thanks be to God in Christ Jesus that our names are written in the Lamb's Book of Life and no one can erase it because it is written in the Precious, Priceless BLOOD of JESUS CHRIST. Not only are our names written in the Lamb's Book of Life, but God is going to write something on us. John confirmed this when he wrote: "Him that overcometh will I make a pillar in the temple of my God, and he shall go no more out: and I will write upon him the name of my God, and the name of the city of my God, which is new Jerusalem, which cometh down out of heaven from my God: and I will write upon him my new name" (Revelation 3:12).

Rahab's story should encourage all of us to know not to let anyone count us out because of the bad choices we have made, the bad paths we have trodden, the bad people we have connected ourselves to, because the Blood of Jesus is powerful and potent enough to save from the gutter-most to the uttermost!

DISTINCT QUALITIES OF GREATNESS

- God Fearing
- Bold
- Brave
- Risk Assessor: Risk Taker
- Able to Formulate Plan of Action
- Unselfish
- Welcoming to Strangers
- Leader
- Entrepreneur

EPILOGUE

WHEN THE STORM BREAKS

You educate a man; you educate a man. You educate a woman you educate a generation. —Mark Twain

As I was in the final stages of writing this manuscript and at the beginning of the editing process, my wife and I saw two films which depicted and epitomized the lives of Great Women. One of the films was ELIZABETH—THE GOLDEN AGE. She was one of England's Great Monarchs. The film depicted a time when Spain was the most powerful empire on earth and her King Philip was a staunch Catholic who plunged the world into a holy war. Only England stood against him with her Protestant Queen. Half the English population were Catholics at the time, so he was attempting to foment dissension against her from within her own country, while he prepared his ships to attack.

As the Spanish Armada of ships were sailing towards the coast of England and the nation was preparing for war, Queen Elizabeth met with her spiritual advisor hoping he could give her some glimmer of hope for victory against the advancing enemy. At one point in tears she asked him, "Give me hope." He replied, "The forces that shape our world are greater than all of us, Majesty, how can I promise they will inspire in your favor even though you are the queen?"

Then he spoke these words which awakened something in her: "But this much I know. When the storm breaks, each man acts in accordance with his own nature. Some are dumb with terror. Some flee. Some hide. And some…spread their wings like eagles and soar on the wind." His words caused her countenance to change. As she arose from a somber and pensive posture, I saw the nature of the eagle rise up in her: She told him he was a very wise man, to which he responded, "You are a very great lady." When the storm breaks in your life, what nature will you act in accordance with; the divine or the defeated, the lion or the beagle, the chicken or the eagle? When the storm breaks, Great Women rise to the occasion; they spread their wings and prepare to soar; they open their mouths and prepare to ROAR! (Rising Over All Roadblocks)

The other awesome film was HIDDEN FIGURES; a film which featured three main characters. Three Great African-American Women who epitomized fortitude and resilience. Katherine Johnson, Dorothy Vaughan and Mary Jackson, were the brilliant minds at NASA who served as the brains behind one of the greatest operations in history: the launch of astronaut John Glenn into orbit which is described as a stunning achievement that restored the nation's confidence, turned around the space race and galvanized the world. An online article in popularmechanics.com states, "Through sheer tenacity, force of will, and intellect, they ensured their stamp on American history even if their story has remained obscured from public view until now." The article went on to state, "While they did the same work as their white counterparts, African-American computers were paid less and relegated to the segregated west section of the Langley campus, where they had to use separate dining and bathroom facilities. They became known as the "West Computers." Despite having the same education, they had to retake college courses they had already passed and were often never considered for promotions or other jobs within NACA." NACA was the name of the space agency until it was changed to NASA in 1958.

• **Katherine Johnson:** a child prodigy who graduated from high school at 14 and from college at 18. A NASA computational research facility in her home town of Hampton, Virginia is named in her honor. She is a recipient of the Presidential Medal of Honor.

• **Dorothy Vaughan:** became NASA's first African-American supervisor and later an expert FORTRAN Programmer.

• **Mary Jackson:** graduated with dual degrees in Math and Physical Science. She was hired to work at Langley in 1951. After several years as a computer, Jackson took an assignment in assisting the senior aeronautical research engineer who encouraged her to become an engineer herself. She needed to take after-work graduate courses held at segregated Hampton High School. Jackson petitioned the City of Hampton to be able to learn next to her white peers. She went on to become NASA's first African-American female engineer.

As I watched the movie, I was astounded and awestruck by the sheer brilliance of these women and the manner in which they persevered and kept striving until they became pioneers, trailblazers and trendsetters.

EPILOGUE

As I exited the theatre, I mentioned to my wife that I could not believe I had never heard or learned about those Great Women in school or any other place. I went to the bathroom before I headed to my car and, while there, I overheard a conversation between two Caucasian gentlemen. One told the other how good the movie was and how he was surprised he had never heard their story.

In the process of editing this book, I was listening to a program called "Fresh Air" on NPR (National Public Radio) where the host Terry Gross was interviewing a former inmate, Susan Burton, about the daunting experience of getting her life back on track after being released from prison. Her story is truly compelling and I was riveted to it as she recounted the tragic events that almost destroyed her, but for her extraordinary resilience and fortitude. As I listened I realized that this woman ranks among the Great Women of modern times. Her greatness is directly attributed to, not only her personal survival, but her willingness to help other women who are marginalized by society; some through self-inflicted wounds, and others who have had wounds inflicted upon them.

Ms. Burton recounted her childhood experiences, which included sexual abuse at age four, gang rape and repeated physical and sexual abuse up to age fourteen. She talked about her 5-year-old son being accidentally killed by a LAPD detective, who did not even get out of his car, and to add to her pain, was not even offered an apology by him nor the police department. She recalled the sight of her son lying dead and being engulfed by anger, rage, and depression, which led to years of alcoholism substance abuse, and ultimately six terms of incarceration.

This phenomenal woman talked about the lack of resources for poor black people during the era of 'War on Drugs' and her struggle to not only break the habits and get her life back on track, but having to internalize her pain until the age of 46. After her final release from prison she resolved to turn her situation around and become an activist for women; to stop recidivism in the lives of other women. Today Susan Burton manages a program where women who have been incarcerated find a safe place to live, receive counseling, and other services that prepare them for reintegration into society. Among her many accomplishments, Ms. Burton founded the organization, 'A New Way of Life', recorded her memoirs in, Becoming Ms. Burton, and was named CNN Hero in 2010. A modern-day hero indeed!

Greatness always finds a way to rise and manifest itself, irrespective of the obstacles it has to overcome. That awesome movie reaffirmed something I've always known: gender and color should not be used to stifle an individual's creativity and opportunity. Each of us should be able to use our mental aptitude and hard work to make our nation and our world a better place. In one of his many hit songs, James Brown sang, "This is a man's world, but it wouldn't be nothing without a woman or a girl." I believe he is right in one part of the song and that is the part where he stated, "The world would be nothing without a woman or a girl." When men stop looking at the world as theirs and recognize we were all placed here by God, both male and female, to work together in unity, regardless of color, class, gender or creed, then the world will not have as much self-centeredness and greed. As men, we cannot allow ourselves to feel threatened by Great Women, but must endeavor to work with them in unison.

I don't believe there has ever been a man who achieved greatness and in retrospect could not name a Great Woman who helped him to achieve that status. A Great Man is a man who is secure enough in who he is to be able to receive from the Great Woman or Women in his life. That man will not allow pride to keep him in a low place when he has help to meet every challenge he will ever face.

In one of his profound teachings, the late Dr. Myles Munroe gave five things a man needs before he gets a woman. Prior to listing the five things he gave a revelation on the Garden of Eden that blessed me tremendously. He said in the Hebrew language, Eden was not just a garden with trees; Eden was a delightful spot. It was not so much a place as it was an atmosphere because it was the Presence of God. When man sinned and was driven out of Eden, it was the Presence of God that he was driven from. Here are the five things a man needs before he gets a woman.

God's Presence—A woman should meet the man in the Presence of God. Dr. Munroe said some women amazed him. They leave the Presence of God, go into the bush and find a brother and try to drag him into the Presence of God. Eve met Adam in the Presence of God.

Work—God gave man work before He gave him woman.

Cultivate—God told man to cultivate. The woman that a man is looking for is in his mind. God never gives a man a finished woman.

The man should take the raw material he married and cultivate it into the woman in his head. If he is not happy with her after twenty years it is because he has not yet cultivated her.

Guard—Man is the protector. He was made stronger with greater muscle mass, not to abuse the woman, but to protect her.

God's Word—God spoke to the man about the tree, not the woman. The man's job was to teach his wife.

When God said it is not good for man to be alone, He was speaking about a man who was in His Presence working, cultivating, protecting, and teaching the word. If you meet a man who is not doing these things, it is good for that man to be alone.

GREAT WOMEN

A LETTER TO MEN—WHERE DO WE GO FROM HERE??

DEAR MEN,

I wrote this book about Great Women, but now, as a man, I'm challenging and putting the onus on myself and other men to take responsibility for making sure the abuse and traumatizing of women ceases. We cannot say we love women, but do little or nothing to end the atrocities so many women face all over the globe. MEN, BROTHERS, Love is a verb; love is an action word, so Great Men must take swift and decisive action against the chauvinistic and misogynistic mindset which fights against the Greatness of Women. We must love women actively and proactively. Men can ill-afford to sit silently on the sidelines while women are the victims of rape, molestation, and domestic violence; while young girls are kidnapped and sold as sex slaves, while they are the victims of honor killings. Silence in the face of atrocities gives tacit approval and makes some men complicit. Brothers we need to become advocates, protectors, and champions of the causes of women; not only our mothers, daughters, sisters, and our nieces but women all over the globe. The fight for women's rights, for equality and justice for all women, on the part of men, must be a global move and it must be proactive, which means, at the very least, men should speak out when they see and hear about injustice towards women. That is how we can become true allies to our sisters in the fight for gender justice locally, nationally and globally.

Advocacy means listening; asking questions to gain greater awareness of the issues women must deal with in patriarchal, male-dominated societies. Once we gain awareness, we must make a decision to take action because indecision can be tantamount to doing nothing. Are you ok with your daughter being paid less than her male counterpart simply because she is a female? When you send her off to college, do you know there is a chance she may become a victim of a sexual assault because sexual assault of young women on college campuses has reached epidemic proportions? In the military, which is another male dominated institution, she needs to be protected from male sexual predators many of whom may be her fellow service-men, even her superiors. Strong men must make their voices heard when it comes to the fight against the trauma many women suffer in society. I am not referring solely to Third world or so-called underdeveloped countries. Women are being traumatized in wealthy industrialized nations like the United States as well.

When Hannah was being tormented and traumatized by her husband's other wife, Peninnah, there is no biblical evidence that her husband attempted to stop it. As a man sworn to protect her from enemies within and without, why didn't he demand that Peninnah put a stop to her incessant traumatizing of Hannah? Men, you must be strong and unrelenting in your advocacy of equal rights and justice for all women. I truly believe a society's moral compass is judged by its treatment of women. When a woman is mistreated it has a ripple effect, not only in her home, but in society at large. A woman who feels safe and secure with no shackles on her feet will be able to contribute greatly to society.

RECIPROCITY

It is time for men to reciprocate. Our first resting place, nesting place, was the womb of the woman who conceived and carried us; cradled us and nourished us in our fetal and embryonic state. She is the carrier of life. She endured the birth pangs, the painful contractions, to bring you into this world. She put her life on the line for you because birthing a baby can put a woman's life at risk of death. Once you came into this world she forgot about her pain, and sacrificed her time, energy, and her finances to give you the best opportunity, not only to survive, but to overcome. Daddy may not be there, but 99.9 percent of the time momma is there through thick and thin. In light of all she has done and continues to do for you, it is unconscionable that she should be relegated to some second class or inferior status in society. She should be held up as the Crowning Jewel of God's Creation.

My wife and I were watching a series called, Z: The Beginning of Everything. The series is an adaptation of a novel about the life of Zelda Fitzgerald, the wife of F Scott Fitzgerald. There is a scene where the couple is returning to Alabama to visit her parents because they have run out of money while living the high life in New York City. Their car broke down in front of the home of a black family when one of the wheels flew off. After the man of the house helped them to put the wheel back on, Zelda Fitzgerald jumped in the driver's seat while her husband occupied the passenger seat. With a shocked look on his face, the man of the house asked F Scott, "You gone let her drive?"—to which F Scott replied respectfully, but firmly—"Why not, she's my queen." Men, women are queens so give them the royal treatment they deserve.

Afterword

I am deeply moved by Apostle Fidel Donaldson's championship of women in this book, Great Women. His decision to speak up for women in the church who may feel silenced by interpretations of the Gospel that suggest that God sees women as second class citizens, is a rare thing to see among male church leaders, but it is an important contribution. Donaldson's book presents a powerful counter-narrative that belies false assumptions that women have no authority to speak, teach or preach on behalf of God's Kingdom. Apostle Donaldson makes a compelling case for female inclusion in church leadership and in every aspect of Kingdom service—from the humblest role to the highest—using Great Women from the Bible to argue convincingly that God has always used women to spread His Word and to do His will on earth. More significantly, Donaldson argues that God rarely chooses women who are well-oiled to do His will. He chooses imperfect women and perfects them for and in service to His will.

As I read Apostle Donaldson's narrative, I kept thinking of one woman from American history who was called by God, and whose story rivals those of many of the women of the Bible about which Apostle Donaldson writes so eloquently. She was also a champion for women's suffrage and an anti-slavery advocate. She is known for the famous question: "Ain't I a Woman?" when her gender was questioned because of her forthrightness and her insistence that she spoke by God's leave and, thus, needed no permission from man to speak in public. Her name was Sojourner Truth.

This Great Woman, Sojourner Truth, was an African-American woman, who was a slave in Ulster County, New York, in the early 19th century before slavery was abolished in New York in 1827. Yes, that's right. There was slavery in some northern states, a historical fact rarely taught in our schools. Her given name was Isabella Bomefree. Her surname was given to her father by their master, a Dutch slave-owner in New York State. When she ran away from slavery, she renamed herself Sojourner Truth. Then, as if to give her name legs, she walked all over New York and Connecticut preaching the Truth of God's existence and power to all who would listen to her. She became a great orator, as renown for her oratorical skills as the great Frederick Douglass, even though she could neither read nor write.

Later, she narrated her story to a white female writer, Olive Gilbert, who published a biography on her life. In the introduction to the book she edited on Sojourner

Truth, Narrative of Sojourner Truth, historian Margaret Washington observes: "Many doors were closed to African-American women in her day, but it was difficult to shut out Sojourner Truth. She was bold and insistent. Her teaching, preaching, and speaking methods; her moving renditions of Methodist hymns and songs of her own creation; her intuitive, universal insights; her unfailing commitment to black progress; and her enduring friendships with erudite American reformers made Sojourner a force in history. She even held audience with two American Presidents on behalf of her people. Scholars, dramatists, schoolchildren, and others in popular circles still recite her speeches, recall her maxims and praise her contributions" (ix)

Sojourner Truth credits her talents and knowledge to her personal relationship to God Almighty Himself. She recounts to Olive Gilbert how her slave-mother, who could neither read nor write herself, taught her children to know God and to go to God in prayer:

"My children, there is a God, who sees and hears you"
A God, mau-mau!" "Where does he live?" asked the children.
"He lives in the sky," she replied; and when you are beaten, or cruelly treated, or fall into any trouble, you
must ask of him, and he will always hear and help you."
She taught them to kneel and say the Lord's Prayer. She entreated them to refrain from lying and stealing and to strive to obey their masters" (7).

With that strong spiritual foundation, Isabella became a force to be reckoned with. She relates the story to Ms. Gilbert of how she came to know Jesus as an intercessor between her and God. After a period of lying, stealing, and committing all the sins her mother warned her against, Isabella could not feel God's presence anymore. The narrative states: "At length a friend appeared to stand between herself and an insulted Deity; and she felt as sensibly refreshed as when, on a hot day, an umbrella had been interposed between her scorching head and a burning sun." When she insisted on knowing who this friend was, for she felt His presence, but did not personally know Jesus, "an answer came to her, saying distinctly, "It is Jesus," "Yes,' she responded, "it is Jesus" (Washington, 50-51).

Prior to this, Isabella had heard the name Jesus but she thought he was just another famous American, like George Washington.

Jesus revealed himself to her one day without anyone teaching her the Bible, or without her hearing of Him in church. In fact, as a slave she was not allowed to attend church. After that, she changed her name to Sojourner Truth, ran away from her master one year before slavery was abolished in New York State, and became such a powerful witness for God that she saved many souls for His Kingdom. One incident in the book recounts how she was able to pacify a gang of rebels who came one night to break up a revival meeting. She was the lone Black person present, but she was the only one whose voice had the power to persuade the gangsters to leave in peace. Sojourner Truth begun to sing a hymn which so touched the mob that they immediately stopped rioting to listen to her voice: "Her speech had operated on the roused passions of the mob like oil on agitated waters; they were, as a whole, entirely subdued, and only clamored when she ceased to speak or sing" (95).

Sojourner Truth is not a Great Woman of the Bible, but she was, nevertheless, a Great Woman of God. She deserves a place in this Hall of Faith for Great Women that the Great Man of God has written. Truth's life and works exemplify one of my favorite scriptures: "For God hath not given us a spirit of fear; but of power, and of love, and of a sound mind." 2 Timothy 1:7.

I believe that this book will inspire the Great Women in the churches, locally and globally, to rise up, shake off the shackles of fear, self-doubt, and false interpretations from patriarchal ideologies that have crept into biblical doctrine, and claim their rightful heritage as daughters of the Most High, God with a righteous and equal claim to the spiritual riches of His Kingdom. Like Sojourner Truth and all the women mentioned in this book, let us speak and act by no other authority above God's and, by His leave, claim our Greatness as women and men conjoined in spiritual partnership to do the will of God.

Dr. Donna Aza Weir-Soley,
Associate Professor of English,
Florida International University

Bibliography

Works Cited

Burton, Susan and Cari Lynn. Becoming Ms. Burton: From Prison to Recovery to Leading the Fight For Incarcerated Women. The New Press, 2017.

Donaldson, Fidel. Midnight. Appeal Ministries, 2010.

Donaldson, Fidel. It's Time to Come Out of Lo-Debar, Appeal Ministries, 2015.

Evans, Patricia. The Verbally Abusive Relationship. Adams Media, 2010.

Hardy, Monica. Embracing God: My Season of Single (unpublished manuscript) 2016, Love, Peace and Joy Ministry/Kingdom Scholastic Center of Excellence.

Jakes, T.D. Woman Thou Art Loosed! Destiny Image Publishers, 2012.

Jamieson, Fausett and Brown's Commentary (Critical and Explanatory on the Whole Bible), 1871. https://biblesoft.com/products/159-jamiesonb00219-jamieson-fausset-brown-s-commentary.html. Accessed February 10, 2016.

Kolk, Bessel van der. The Body Keeps the Score. Penguin Books, 2014.

Melfi, Theodore, director. Hidden Figures., Twentieth Century Fox, 2016.

Munroe, Myles. Understanding the Purpose and Power of Woman. Whitaker House, 2001.

Schuessler, Axel. ABC Etymological Dictionary of Old Chinese. University of Hawaii Press, 2007.

Spangler, Ann and Syswerda, Jean E. Women of the Bible. Zondervan, 2007.

Washington, Margaret, ed. Narrative of Sojourner Truth. Vintage Books, 1993.

Yaeger, Don. Greatness: The 16 Characteristics of True Champions. Center Street Books, 2011.

Z: The Beginning of Everything. Directed by Tim Blake Nelson, Mike Barker, Minko Spiro. Amazon Studios, 2015-2017.

Further Suggested Readings

Barnett, O.W., and A.D. LaViolette. It Could Happen to Anyone: Why Battered Women Stay. Sage Publication, 1993.

Jacobs, Harriet A. Incidents in the Life of a Slave Girl. Edited and with an introduction by Jean Fagan Yellin, Harvard University Press, 2000.

Jeffers, Susan. Feel the Fear and Do It Anyway. Ballantine Books, 1987.

Ross, Ruth. Prospering Woman: A Complete Guide to Achieving the Full, Abundant Life. Whatever Publishing, Inc., 1982.

Sinetar, Marsha. Do What You Love, the Money Will Follow: Discovering Your Right Livelihood, Paulist Press, 1987.

Stoddard, Alexandra. Living a Beautiful Life. Random House, Inc., 1986.

National Hotlines and Helpful Links

VictimConnect
National Hotline for Crime Victims
1-855-4-VICTIM (1-855-484-2846)

Office for Victims of Crime, Directory of Crime Victim Services
National Suicide Prevention Lifeline
1-800-273-TALK (8255) [24/7 hotline]
1-888-628-9454 (Spanish)
1-800-799-4889 (TTY)

Disaster Distress Helpline [24/7 hotline]
1-800-985-5990

FINRA Securities Helpline for Seniors
844-57-HELPS

Gift from Within
207.236.8858

Identity Theft Resource Center
1-888-400-5530
Internet Crime Complaint Center
Jennifer Ann's Group
Free resources on teen dating violence

MADD (Mothers Against Drunk Driving)
1-800-438-6233

National Alliance on Mental Illness
1-800-950-6264

National Association of Crime Victim Compensation Boards
[links to every state's compensation program]

National Center on Elder Abuse
National Child Abuse Hotline
1-800-422-4453

National Coalition of Anti-Violence Programs,
National Advocacy for Local LGBT Communities
1-212-714-1141

National Domestic Violence Hotline
1-800-799-7233 or 1-800-787-3224 (TTY)

National Indigenous Women's Resource Center
406-477-3896

National Runaway Switchboard
1-800-786-2929

National Sexual Assault Hotline
1-800-656-4673 [24/7 hotline]

National Teen Dating Abuse Helpline
1-866-331-9474 or 1-866-331-8453 (TTY)

Overseas Citizens Services
1-888-407-4747
1-202-501-4444 (from overseas)

Parents of Murdered Children
1-888-818-7662

LGBT Youth Crisis & Suicide Prevention Hotline
1-866-488-7386

The Trauma Center at JRI www.traumacenter.org

HelpPro Therapist Finder HTTP://www.helppro.com

The Recovered Memory Project http://www.brown.edu/academics/taubman-center/.

Office for Victims of Crime in the Department of Justice http://ojp.gov/ovc/.

National Institute of Mental Health http://www.nimh.nih.gov/health/topics/post-traumatic-stress-disorder-ptsd/index.shtml

National Child Traumatic Stress Network (NCTSN) http://nctsnet.org